How Far Can We Go?

A Catholic Guide to Sex and Dating

Leah Perrault *and* Brett Salkeld
Foreword by Ronald Rolheiser, OMI

Paulist Press
New York/Mahwah, NJ

Dedication

For the many people whose generous gifts of self
have been God's presence in our lives,
challenging us to be and become disciples of Jesus,
especially for Marc and Flannery.

NIHIL OBSTAT:
Reverend Monsignor James M. Cafone, S.T.D.
Censor Librorum

May 18, 2011

IMPRIMATUR:
+ Most Rev. John J. Myers, D.D., J.C.D.
Archbishop of Newark

May 20, 2011

The Nihil Obstat and Imprimatur are official declarations that a book or pamphlet is free of doctrinal or moral error. No implication is contained therein that those who have granted the Nihil Obstat and Imprimatur agree with the contents, opinions or statements expressed.

Cover design by Sharyn Banks

First published in 2009 by Novalis Publishing Inc., Canada

Library of Congress Cataloging-in-Pubication Data

Perrault, Leah.
    How far can we go? : a Catholic guide to sex and dating / Leah Perrault and Brett Salkeld.
        p. cm.
    "First published in 2009 by Novalis Publishing Inc., Canada."
    ISBN 978-0-8091-4726-7 (alk. paper)
    1. Sex—Religious aspects—Catholic Church. 2. Sex instruction—Religious aspects—Catholic Church. 3. Dating (Social customs)—Religious aspects—Catholic Church. I. Salkeld, Brett. II. Title.
    BX1795.S48P48 2010
    241'.6765088282—dc22

                                                                          2010045365

Published by Paulist Press
997 Macarthur Boulevard
Mahwah, New Jersey 07430

www.paulistpress.com

Printed and bound in the
United States of America

Contents

Foreword

by Ronald Rolheiser

When I was a teenager, neither my father nor my mother ever sat me down for a serious one-to-one talk about sex. That was not their style. Sex wasn't talked about as openly then as it is today. But neither did they abdicate their role and leave me to the whims of the culture to learn about sex. My mother gave me a series of pamphlets she picked up from the local church library. While these may have lacked the sophistication of some of the contemporary literature on dating and sexuality, they did indelibly stamp a fundamental truth into my young soul: *Sex is good and sex is sacred, but it is only good and sacred when it is linked to a lifelong commitment within marriage.*

I have studied a lot of psychology, anthropology and theology since that time, and, during nearly 40 years of priesthood, I have listened to many people, young and old, share how they have been wounded through sexual relationships that initially promised to be life-giving but ended up bringing chaos and bitterness into their lives. As a result, I am more convinced than ever of the truth about sex that I learned from those old church pamphlets that my mother gave me as a teenager: *Don't go to bed with anyone to whom you aren't married.*

There is an old joke about sex that unwittingly carries that lesson. The question is: "What does a promiscuous person do after having sex?" The answer: "He or she goes home!" That line teaches a deep truth: sex is meant to be home! If you have to go home after having sex with someone, then you shouldn't be having it, because there is something not right when you give yourself so totally to someone with whom you are unwilling to share your home. Moreover, to have to go home *from* someone with whom you have just shared this kind of intimacy triggers either a deep emptiness or an unhealthy hardness inside us. We see this most clearly in its extreme form, the singles bar. To pick up someone for anonymous sex is a schizophrenic act, an act that takes you outside of yourself and outside of your home. From such an act, you eventually need to go back home. The same is ultimately true for all sex outside of marriage. You eventually need to go home – in either emptiness or hardness of soul.

How Far Can We Go? A Catholic Guide to Sex and Dating is much more sophisticated than the pamphlets my mother gave me as a teenager, but its message is the same: sex is good and sex is sacred, but only when it is linked to a lifelong commitment within marriage. Again and again, the authors return to this fundamental principle – and it is a sound principle, one on which you can stake your life and love. Their moral and psychological exactitude is invariably excellent. For example, each of these axioms, quotes from their text, might be from a morality or psychology textbook:

- *Sex is not a shortcut to intimacy! If you want to have sex but don't want to get married, you need to look at your reason for not getting married. If it's not a very good reason, work through it and get married. If it's a good reason, then it's probably a good reason not to have sex.*
- *Any good reason why you are unable to promise your life to someone is a good reason not to have sex with that someone.*

They engage all the major questions surrounding sex and young people with a disarming honesty and a language that, if it has a fault, is too blunt, and on each question show where the Catholic moral compass lands. And their guidelines are not simplistic, either morally or psychologically. They bring to bear what is both timeless and best inside of Catholic moral tradition, even as they remain sensitive to what we have learned from the best insights of the human sciences.

This is a needed book: since the dawn of civilization, virtually every culture has had major taboos about sex. Sex has been, almost without exception, linked to marriage. Our own culture, for the most part, has severed that link. Today, sex is generally seen as an extension of dating. The common view is that sex can legitimately take place before marriage, if love is there, and that sex can be resacralized and made monogamous after marriage. We live in a culture that believes we can experiment with sex until we find the right person to marry, and then bring sex "home" and live it out more traditionally.

There is too little literature available that isn't overly simplistic or overly casual and that challenges us on sex. Generally, the literature on sex tends to deny either some of the complexities of sexuality or the seriousness and the consequences of irresponsible sex. This book walks that fine line between the overly simplistic and the overly casual.

It affirms that sex is always partially beyond us, too powerful to contain easily. It takes seriously the brute power of sex and points out that it is both the most creative and the most destructive force on the planet. It is a great force not just for heroic love, life and blessing, but also for the worst hate, death and destruction imaginable. It is responsible for most ecstasies on the planet, but also for countless murders and suicides. When healthy, it helps glue personalities together; when unhealthy, it works at disintegrating personalities. It can unite families and communities, or it can destroy them. It has a unique power to mellow the heart and produce gratitude, even as it has equal power to make the heart bitter and jealous. It is the best of all fires and the most dangerous of all fires.

And so, these young authors point out, it is important to admit that sex is a power beyond us even as we accept that we have a responsibility to control it; that its goodness must always be affirmed, even as its dangers are highlighted; that its sacred character should always be taught, even as its earthiness should never be denigrated; that we must be clear that it is meant to be sacrament, even as it is meant to be playful; that it is meant to bring children into this world, even as it is meant to express love; that it is meant to be healthily enjoyed, even as it needs to be carefully guarded; and that it is not something before which we should stand in unhealthy fear, even as we surround it with enough taboos to properly safeguard its meaning and our own emotional safety.

Sex might be compared to a high-voltage electrical wire. The 50,000 volts inside of that wire can bring light and heat to a home, but there are two risks. First, we may be so afraid of its dangers that we never connect our house to it. We deprive ourselves of its light and heat. Second, to harness this energy wisely, we must access its raw power through the appropriate channels, with proper safeguards in place. Otherwise, we risk a deadly fire.

So … how far can we go? Where is that fine line between being overly fearful and overly careless about sex? How do we avoid frigidity on the one hand and heartbreak on the other? This book, drawing upon centuries of moral and human wisdom, is a healthy guide.

Ronald Rolheiser OMI
Oblate School of Theology
San Antonio, Texas
March 28, 2009

Introduction

For the young Catholics we meet, few issues are as interesting or as significant as Catholic teaching about sexuality. In the best cases, young Catholics are talking about faith and sexuality with enthusiasm and many questions. In the worst cases, Catholics of all ages think that the Catholic word on sex is simply "no." As Catholics, we have been asked to explain Catholic understandings on these issues more than any other; in life, we are taking up the challenge to live these teachings with joy.

The first time we met, we spent hours discussing this very topic. Leah was unconvinced about the Catholic position on artificial contraception. Brett was doing his best to explain it to her.

Brett's Catholic upbringing was uneven. Though his mother got the family to Mass every Sunday, they were not always happy to be there. Brett himself went through a period of unhappy atheism; his father left the Church to join an evangelical Protestant community, eventually returning to Catholicism with a more mature and explicit faith.

By the time he left home to attend university, Brett was convinced of the truth of the Catholic faith. At university, people challenged him on his faith constantly. Evangelical friends had concerns about Catholic practices such as praying to the saints or going to confession. Others, Catholics and non-Catholics, rejected Church teaching on sexuality. To continue to affirm Church teaching in these areas, Brett needed to know more about what the Church actually said. This is where his work in sexual ethics began. By the time Brett met Leah, he was the person in the Catholic student group on campus to whom such questions were directed.

Leah was raised in an active Catholic family. She loved participating in the life of the parish. When she was a teenager, Catholic youth programming in rural Saskatchewan was limited, so she joined an (evangelical) Alliance Church Bible Quizzing program. She was excited to discover hundreds of Christian youth who were committed to living their faith. Leah became confused about the Catholic Church and was not sure where to find answers. She arrived at university looking for a church community whose spirituality she could understand intellectually and live with enthusiasm. Brett was one of many people who helped Leah to hear God calling her to faith within the Catholic Church. When she met Brett, Leah's concerns about birth control led to that first long talk with him. (We have had countless conversations since then. Now that we are both married, although not to each other, the conversations continue.)

In time (and with grace), Leah joined Brett as one of the Catholic student leaders on campus. In the later years of university, our friends (many of whom were also Catholic student leaders) at school and in ministry began to ask us to speak about faith at youth retreats, to confirmation classes and in parishes. What has become Tobias and Sarah Ministries began when our friend Lisette asked Brett to speak to a group of World Youth Day pilgrims. They hadn't chosen a topic, hoping Brett could come up with something he'd like to talk about. Lisette told Brett that one of the parents had reluctantly agreed to speak about sexuality, but the rest of the program was wide open. "Reluctantly?" thought Brett. "Who wouldn't want to speak to a room full of teenagers about sex?"

When Lisette heard that Brett would like to discuss this topic, she informed the relieved parent and a date was set for the gathering. Brett immediately called Leah to ask if she'd like to help with this project, and the first "sex talk" was born. That presentation was over three hours, with no scheduled breaks. Though everyone enjoyed the talk, we left with many ideas for improving it.

Since that first gathering, we have developed two presentations – one on dating and one on marriage – which we usually give consecutively. We have given these presentations primarily to teens and young adults, but we have also spoken to parents, teachers, clergy, colleagues and friends. As you are about to discover, our message is about more than dating. Our message is about being and becoming a son or daughter of God. Though our audiences have been predominantly Catholic, some non-Catholics who have attended have found our work helpful for their own faith. We offer a way of thinking about spirituality and sexuality from a Catholic perspective, but it is our conviction and our hope that some of our insights might be helpful for people beyond the Catholic Church as well.

Neither of us thought that our presentations would one day turn us into published authors, but each time we are invited to speak, people ask us for something comprehensive to take home and share with a friend or family member, because some aspect of what we have said has touched them. Perhaps a video, a recording, a book?

This is our book. We hope you enjoy it.

Leah and Brett

A Note for Parents, Teachers and Pastors

When we began to give our presentations, we were a lot more like your children, students or youth. We were students. We were single. We were closer to their age than yours. And we were asking, "How far can we go?" as we ourselves were trying to navigate the journey from stranger to spouse in our lives.

Now, we are perhaps a bit more like you than like the youth in our lives. We are graduate students and eager learners. We are formally employed in Catholic ministry. We are married (though not to each other) and the parents of young children. And, like you, we have great hope for a future Church that includes all the young people in our lives.

As young Catholics, we began with a look at Catholic teaching on sexuality and marriage. We asked ourselves how we might prepare for marriage, if that was where we were called. In some ways, there is no preparing for the adventure that is marriage … but there are a great many ways to prepare for the relationships that will make up whatever vocation God has in store for us.

This book is not a magic solution to prevent youth from making mistakes in dating and relationships. The heart of the wisdom we have discovered in Catholic teaching on sexuality is that we are called to understand and respect the dignity of each and every human person, since all are created in the image of God. Our approach to dating and marriage in the pages that follow is to help young people to understand themselves and the people around them.

We prefer to speak to teens with their parents and pastors present. We find that this approach fosters greater discussion about sexuality at home and beyond the evenings we spend speaking to youth. More significantly, parents, teachers and pastors have told us that they feel under-equipped to help their young people develop a Catholic attitude towards sexuality. This book can help you. As a parent, pastor, teacher or friend, you are an essential person in the life of some young Catholics. We believe that your faith, support and advice can have a positive influence on the values and choices of young people. Though our book is aimed at young people, we hope that you will also read it, finding in these pages a language and wisdom that you can relate to and share with the young people in your life.

Leah and Brett

1

Why We Had to Write This Book ⟳

You can't jump off a cliff with both feet on the floor … or something like that. If you've been asking questions about dating in the Catholic Church, you may have heard something about feet or cliffs. Here are two famous answers to the question "How far can we go?":

- Keep both feet on the floor.
- Asking "How far can we go?" is like taking your girlfriend or boyfriend in your arms, walking to the edge of a cliff, and asking, "How close can I get to the edge?"

We had to write this book because we think both these answers are unsatisfactory. We think we can do better. The first answer is very practical, but anyone with a little imagination can get around it. In trying to set out an easy-to-follow guideline for Catholic couples, it ignores the question of Christian formation. It says that physical intimacy is only about how you act, and has no connection to the kind of person you are called to be and to become.

The second answer is much more dangerous. The foundation of the metaphor it uses is that sex is roughly equivalent to suicide! In other words, sex is dangerous and sinful. Any advance in physical intimacy is just getting you closer and closer to the edge of the cliff. When we give answers like this, it is no wonder the world thinks the Church is down on sex. (We'll talk more about both these answers in Chapter 3.)

In reality, the Church and the world basically agree: sex is good – very good! The difference between the Church's attitude towards sex and the world's attitude towards sex stems from a disagreement about *why* sex is good.

The world thinks sex is good because it is pleasurable. The world also thinks sex is necessary, because most healthy human persons have, for at least part of their lives, strong sex drives. The attitude that sex is good and necessary because it is pleasurable and fulfills a natural drive means that sex is, at the same time, the most important thing and the least important thing. It is so important that sometimes we are told that people who live without it are bound to go nuts, but it is so unimportant that it isn't always necessary to know the name of the person you engage in it with.

The Church, on the other hand, says that sex is so important, it must be engaged in with the greatest respect both for sex itself and for your partner; but sex is not so important that you will die or become mentally unstable if you aren't having it. If we are to understand the Church's position on sex and dating, we need to understand why the Church thinks sex is good in the first place.

The world is right: sex is good because it is pleasurable. But that is not the whole story! For a Christian, sex is good, first of all, because it is part of God's good creation. God made us male and female and saw that it was good! It is part of the nature of humanity that we are built to be in relationship with one another. The story in Genesis says that Adam was lonely until God made a partner for him. God's gift of sexuality calls us out of ourselves and into relationship with our fellow human beings. Furthermore, part of our call to grow in holiness is realized when we recognize the good that God did in creating those around us. And the pleasure of sex is part of a larger and deeper joy that we find in God's gifts to us. Our sexuality calls us to see those with whom God puts us in relationship as part of God's good creation. In fact, the basic affirmation of the Christian faith is that, in order to restore our relationship with him, God himself took on a body and became one of us, sexuality and all.

Sex is good because it is the culmination of the language of physical intimacy. That language gives us a unique and powerful way to communicate about our relationships with one another. It is a language that both speaks the truth about our relationships and reinforces that truth. When it is used to honestly communicate the truth about any of our relationships (with parents, friends, teammates, boyfriends, girlfriends or spouses), physical intimacy serves to enhance all the other areas of our relationships.

One of the reasons that Christian books on sex and dating have given a misleading view about sexuality is that they ignore the essential communicative aspect of sexuality. Sexual sin is presented as crossing some vague boundary partway up an imaginary list of increasingly intimate physical acts. But, in the context of physical intimacy, sin isn't crossing an arbitrary line. Sexual sin is using your body to lie to your partner (and probably yourself) about the nature of your relationship. There need to be one or two clear lines about what is appropriate for unmarried people, but those lines are not drawn to keep people from acts that are impure in and of themselves. They are drawn to keep people from lying with the language of their bodies. This book, then, is not primarily about which acts are and are not permissible. This book is about learning to speak the truth with your body.

We chose the title of this book for two reasons. First, this is the number one question young people ask us when we present the Church's teaching on sexuality. Chapters 2 to 8 of this book deal with dating relationships. A major concern for unmarried people in romantic relationships is this: Which ways of expressing my affection physically are acceptable, and which are not? This concern is usually phrased as "How far can we go?"

Second, because you don't stop asking this question on your wedding day, Chapters 9 to 12 of this book deal with Christian marriage. For a Christian, the question "How far can we go?" really means "*In what way am I being called to give of myself in this relationship?*" That is a question that married people must never stop asking.

What, exactly, is a vocation?

A vocation is a calling from God. Even though we might not be called to be a priest or nun, every person is called into a relationship with God. Our calling to be part of God's very life is our first and foundational vocation. The Church celebrates this vocation when it welcomes people into the Church in baptism. Over the course of our lives, we discern how God is calling us to live in each and every moment. Mature disciples of Jesus discern their vocation all the time! At some point in life, we will be called to choose a permanent "lifestyle" vocation – that is, a way of living our adult discipleship in the world. You might be called to single life, religious life, the priesthood or marriage. Once you've discerned a lifestyle vocation with the help of your family, friends and Church community, you continue to discern how to live out God's call for your life as a single person, priest, religious brother or sister, or spouse/parent. These ways of living in the world offer us many different relationships within which God refines us and makes us holy. The good news is that God never stops calling us!

The subtitle of the book is also important. Yes, the book is about sex and dating (if not at the same time), but it is also "A Catholic Guide." All three words are very important here. First, it is written by two Catholics who have studied the Catholic theological and ethical tradition and want to present something that applies the wisdom of that tradition to the lives of young people today. Second, it is a guide. We want to give people the information they need to make their own decisions, not to make those decisions for them. Finally, it is "a" guide, not "the" guide. Dating is a fairly new thing in Western culture. For the first 1,900 years or so of Christian history, no one had heard of dating. For this reason, and others, the Church has no official teaching about dating. You won't find anything on this topic in the *Catechism of the Catholic Church*. What we present is a guide to applying the Church's teaching on human persons, sexuality and physical intimacy to your relationships.

Dating, courting, special friends?

You might notice throughout our book that we don't make a big deal about using the word "dating" to describe the discernment of marriage relationships. This is because we think Christians are called to witness to the world by their actions. Holy dating can be a powerful way to speak about God's plan for relationships! If calling the process of discernment something else is more comfortable for you, we encourage you to use the words that work for you. How you do it is much more important than what you call it.

We will look at official Church teaching on several topics, such as sex before marriage, pornography, and artificial birth control. We do this for two reasons. First, we want to present Church teaching to you in a clear and convincing way. We want to give the best wisdom we have found for what the Church teaches in these areas. But it is not our intention to make people who disagree with us, or who have not always lived up to God's call in their lives, feel guilty or bad. None of us – the authors of this book included – have always lived up to God's call in the way we live out our sexuality. Think of this book as an invitation. We believe that God has a purpose for you that includes your sexuality, and we want to help you live out that purpose. What you may have done in the past is not the issue. What matters is what God has planned for your future!

Our sexuality is a gift from God. Just as in every other area of our lives, we are invited to become more Christ-like in living out the gift of our sexuality. Our challenge as Christian people is to take Christ with us everywhere, to act with integrity in every situation, to allow God to touch us and transform us in every one of these places. If this is going to happen, we cannot separate parts of ourselves from the loving touch of God.

In dating, we take time to get to know another whole person. We learn to love all of the different aspects of them, to be changed by them, and to figure out how God is calling both of us to serve him in the world. When we date in a way that draws us, individually and together, into a deeper relationship with God, we discover how God is present in each other and in the world around us. God desires for our sexuality to be one more place where we find God and God finds us.

2

The Truth About People and Sex ⊚

If you're dating, we hope you're not having sex. The Church hopes you're not having sex. Our God hopes you will choose to take this time to get to know one another – to discern God's call for your lives while you still have the opportunity to take separate paths, without dealing with the consequences of sex.

Sex is both a sign and a source of married commitment and unity. People who are married are visibly joined to one another in our world. They live in the same home, drive the same car, attend social gatherings with each other, make important decisions together, and are parents to their children. For married people, having sex is a sign and a confirmation of their commitment to one another. We might even think of married sex as the renewal of marriage vows. Many actions in marriages can express these vows – things like choosing to care for a sick spouse, or refusing to consider an affair when the marriage is difficult or lonely. Sex also speaks a language and gives witness to the kind of relationship that exists between two people.

Just as sex is a sign of the love between two people, it is also a source of that love. Because we can never be just physical people, our physical actions have emotional, social, intellectual and spiritual consequences. When two people have sex, they really do "make" love. Entering into sex in all its vulnerability, depth and desire to give yourself and receive your spouse creates and nurtures an amazing bond between two people. Sex makes people physically vulnerable with their spouse; it is also makes them emotionally, spiritually and intellectually vulnerable. It opens up the most intimate places in their hearts, creating compassion for their weaknesses and calling forth courage to face difficulties. Spiritually, married people become "one flesh" in their married life. The closeness and vulnerability of sexual intimacy is a beautiful image of the two becoming one.

The difference between "protection" and "vulnerability"

Sometimes, we are very protective of ourselves or of the people we love. It is human to be cautious, out of concern that things could turn out badly if we aren't careful. Yet, as we grow into deep and meaningful relationships, a healthy amount of caution must give way to trust in the other person. We never have to protect ourselves from someone who loves us deeply. We go to them with openness and vulnerability, to be transformed and loved in ways we had never imagined possible. When it comes to the most intimate physical expressions of love, we should never have to "protect" ourselves from either our partner or the consequences of our loving actions. "Safe sex" is a contradiction: God created sex to be part of a deep and vulnerable relationship, in which two people travel the road to holiness together.

In case you haven't heard, the Catholic Church teaches that sex before marriage is wrong. It's not our mission in life to tell you this. If you're reading this book, you probably already know it, and you might even agree with the Church. Lots of people have said it before. Instead, we hope that, as you think about and live out your sexuality, this book can help you understand *why* the Church teaches that sex belongs in marriage.

Now, you may be thinking, "Sexuality? I thought I wasn't supposed to be having sex!" Actually, sexuality isn't the same thing as sex. When you fill out a form and it asks what your sex is, you don't write "often," "yes, please," or "not yet, thanks." The form is asking if you are male or female. Sexuality does not equal sexual intercourse. Sexuality is about being created for relationships with others. Our creation as male and female is a sign of our being created for relationships. Even though you are not having sex, you are still sexual.

So that's why we can talk about your sexuality even if you're not having sex. The Church cares about sexuality because it cares about humanity. For the Church, sexuality is important because every human person is sexual.

What is a human person? As far as we know, a human person is the only creature in creation that has both a physical body and a rational soul. Angels have rational souls, but no bodies; camels, armadillos and elephants have physical bodies, but no rational souls. Since sex requires a body, angels are out of luck; they won't find any Church teaching on angel sex. Since any sort of moral action requires a rational soul, animals are incapable of moral choices. For example, if a hungry lion kills an antelope, it has done nothing morally wrong (or morally right, for that matter). The lion might make a choice about what it eats, but it cannot one day decide to become a vegetarian.

The Church has teachings about human sexuality because humans are the only creatures that can both have sex and make moral decisions. Sexual decision-making is a uniquely human experience.

Having both bodies and souls shapes the way humans experience one another and the world. We are physical and spiritual beings. But we are also social, emotional and intellectual beings. Human emotion, intellect, and social interaction involve both your body and your soul.

Think of a time when you felt an emotion. Perhaps a friend told a lie about you or betrayed you. When you heard about it, you burst into tears or punched a wall. You heard it with your ears, and cried with your eyes or struck something with your fist. Your soul feels the emotional hurt and acts through the body. Your intellect is involved, too. You understand the difference between lies and truth, between loyalty and betrayal. You think about how you will respond to your friend. Your relationship with that friend, with the person who told you about the lie, and with anyone who saw your response show that you are a social being in a social context. All these aspects – physical, spiritual, emotional, social and intellectual – make us *whole people*. They are key aspects of our humanity.

You may never have thought about how the Church treats us as whole people. If you've been to Mass lately, you've probably noticed some of the ways that your whole self is invited to be involved in worship. When you arrive at the church, you dip your hand in the holy water and cross yourself – a physical sign of your baptism and spiritual membership in the Body of Christ. The readings and the homily invite you to listen and to think (to use your intellect) about how your life relates to God and to others. You turn to your neighbour during the sign of peace, showing that your spirituality is social. Sometimes the music, the homily or receiving the Eucharist may make you feel emotional; wedding and funeral liturgies definitely capture the emotional aspects of spirituality. Perhaps most obviously, Mass has a spiritual component – you have come to worship God.

Marriage is a sharing of two whole people – spiritually, physically, emotionally, socially and intellectually. When a man and a woman are joined in the sacrament of marriage, two whole people give their whole selves as gifts to each other. And they both receive that full gift of self from their spouse. This whole self-gift might remind us of another gift of self: the gift that is celebrated at every Mass. Jesus says, "This is my body, given up for you." When Jesus offers his body on the cross, he offers more than a physical gift. His very life, his thoughts, his feelings, and his desire to know and worship God and to serve others – all of these are contained in his sacrifice.

Jesus came to us, fully God and fully human, and offered his whole self for humanity in his life and ministry. This gift becomes especially clear in the crucifixion and resurrection, where Jesus' gift of his very life became the way for us to share in eternal life. As we offer our whole selves to another person in marriage, marriage becomes a particular path for us to follow Jesus' self-giving. We, too, are made holy by "emptying" ourselves for the sake of others (Philippians 2).

Sometimes, when we are introducing our talks about sexuality, we like to say that they are useful for anyone with half a reproductive system. While you breathe and digest on your own, you cannot reproduce on your own. It is written into our biology that we are made for relationships. In *The Theology of the Body*, Pope John Paul II reminds us that the meaning of the human body is "spousal." He means that human persons find their fulfillment and salvation in relationships of self-giving. This is true for each and every one of us, at every stage of our lives.

As children, we find great joy in discovering the world. Have you ever noticed how quickly a baby learns that smiling, babbling and playing brings joy to others? Have you noticed how a small child reaches out to comfort someone who is crying? As people, we are fulfilled by our gifts of self to others – and we become more like Jesus when we offer ourselves as gifts. We begin practising this self-giving as babies. Our parents, families and communities teach us the value of serving one another. As we grow into children, teens and young adults, we continue to be called by God to offer our gifts to build the kingdom of God by reaching out to those in need. Whether we are called to marriage, religious life or single life, our vocation will be a call to offer ourselves to God and to others in a variety of relationships.

Marriage is a lifelong gift of one whole person to another whole person. The gift of self we offer and receive in our relationships with friends, neighbours, parishioners or strangers may be for a short time, for a certain situation, or it may be a partial gift. But the gift of self we offer to and receive from our spouse in marriage is unique because it is exclusive, total and permanent. And yet, this self-giving spills over and serves the whole world.

Sex belongs in marriage because it is the most complete physical gift we can offer. It is the most intimate experience that two whole people can share. If hugs and kisses from family and friends are a good thing, then sex with your spouse is a fantastically good thing.

Of course, sex is not merely a physical gift. Sex between whole people is also spiritual. In Genesis, we read that when we marry, we leave our parents and cling to our spouse, and the two become "one flesh" (Genesis 2:24). We've never met any married people whose bodies were fused together permanently as a result of their sexual relationship, but in Christian marriage, we are spiritually joined by our commitment to one another. Sex is a powerful spiritual sign and actual source of the unity that makes spouses "one flesh."

The gift of self in sex is also emotional – sex is unifying, joyful, relaxing and fun.

It is also intellectual, because it has meaning, and that meaning can vary. Sometimes sex is a profound act of forgiveness or a grateful thank you. Sometimes sex has a meaning that is beyond our ability to name and analyze.

The gift of sex has a social dimension, too. Perhaps a baby is the most obvious sign that sex changes our community! When we get married, our parents become parents-in-law to our spouse. Our friendships tend to increase or change as two sets of friends merge. Eventually, our parents will likely become grandparents and our siblings will become aunts and uncles.

As you can see, treating sex as merely physical misunderstands the mystery and power of our sexuality. And treating sex as merely physical treats another person as merely physical, as something less than a whole person.

In popular culture, the goodness of sex is often reduced to its capacity to give pleasure. In the mind of the Church, sex does a lot more for people than give them orgasms. As good as orgasms are, the Church insists that sex is good because it is a physical sign of the giving and receiving between two *whole* people in marriage. Sex opens spouses to each other. Sex affirms and reaffirms their commitment. Sex provides for the future of the family and the community. Sex celebrates the life-giving generosity of God and the goodness of creation. This is the kind of sex that the Church desires for you. The best sex ever simply isn't possible outside of the full self-giving offered in marriage – no matter how good it feels physically.

In order to have the kind of sexual relationships that God longs for us to have, we need to be willing to risk ourselves by giving everything we have for the sake of our partner. This journey is exciting, challenging, unpredictable and always accompanied by God and others. The road to everlasting life cannot be taken up with one foot never leaving my front door. Sex speaks a powerful language of love and commitment – and we are called to speak this language honestly and appropriately. Simply put, sex was never intended to be experienced as less than a full gift between two people who love each other. When it comes to great sex, there are no back-up plans, no ejector seats, no shortcuts.

3

There's Gotta Be More Than "Don't do it ..."

Everyone knows that there are dozens (maybe more) of ways to express affection for someone physically. You can probably guess how many of those are sex. That's right, just the one! Some of these ways resemble sex more closely than others. Some of them are appropriate with people who are "just friends" and some aren't. Some you'd do in front of your grandma, and some you wouldn't. The point is that most of us often don't know which expressions of intimacy are okay for non-married people.

You won't be surprised to learn that we aren't the first people who have ever tried to answer this question. The problem is that a lot of the other answers weren't satisfying for the young people we met. (We were unmarried people at the time, and these answers didn't satisfy us, either.)

Now, several years and many presentations later, we still find that most young people are asking, "How far can we go?" They are not asking this question to see how much they can "get away with." They are asking it because they have a deep desire to honour God and one another with their bodies, but the road between a handshake and the gift of sex is vast and unknown. Before we give you our answer to the question in the next chapter, here are two unsatisfying answers that were given to us.

The "How pure can we be?" Model

In response to the question "How far can we go?" we have often heard something like this: "That's the wrong question. The right question for people who are dating is 'How pure can we be?'" The practical guidance that follows this answer usually suggests that non-married people do practically nothing that is physically intimate.

This "answer" is unsatisfying for a couple of reasons. First, it doesn't really help couples to make any practical decisions about physical intimacy. For example, Bart and Erica are in high school. They like each other and would like to date each other. As young Catholics, they want to do things right. They go to Shara, the youth minister at their church, and ask, "How far can we go?" Shara tells them she's excited that they're interested in each other, then says, "I'll let you in on a little secret. Your relationship will do much better if, instead, you ask yourselves how pure you can be." Bart and Erica look at each other, a bit confused, then look back at Shara with blank stares. "So, can we hold hands, or what?!"

Learning about appropriate and holy physical intimacy is important in all relationships. Babies need to be touched to learn that they are loved and to learn how to speak. We teach children to give high fives and to differentiate between good and bad touches. Strangers shake hands; if strangers become friends, they might hug or kiss in greeting. Families negotiate boundaries of physical intimacy. For example, the first time Leah went home to visit Marc's family, Marc kissed everyone on the lips. By the third time Leah visited, Marc's mom, dad, grandparents, and aunts and uncles were kissing *her* on the lips. In Leah's family, only married people kiss on the lips – so this took some getting used to. It also changed the meaning of a brief kiss on the lips for Leah and Marc! Learning how to set personal boundaries, and boundaries for different social settings and types of relationships, is an important skill. The "How pure can we be?" response does not help people set these kinds of boundaries.

Second, this "answer" does not define purity well. It implies that any expression of physical intimacy is impure. And, if you tell yourself for a few years of dating that physical intimacy is bad, this negative association with sex will be hard to reverse when you find yourself in bed for the first time with your spouse! Even for a couple that arrives at the honeymoon suite thinking sex is good, the leap from as little physical intimacy as possible to its fullest expression in one day is a bit much.

A woman we know who went to a Catholic boarding school in the 1960s remembers watching a film in class about relationships. A young engaged couple was on a date. When the gentleman dropped off the young lady at her home, he bid her good evening by shaking her hand. Not even a brief hug. Our friend was scandalized. As she said, "I'm not going to shake hands with a guy one night and spread my legs for him the next!" The jump from shaking hands, which you would do with a complete stranger, to lovemaking was simply too jarring. Even if you know someone really well, some growth in physical intimacy must help you make a transition from shaking hands to having sex.

In Chapters 1 and 2, we said that sex is good. Really good. And so are our bodies. The way you feel when someone you love gives you a hug, when your teachers, coaches or parents pat you on the back to tell you how proud they are of your latest accomplishment, or when your teammate high fives you after you make a shot in a basketball game shows how your body plays an important role in sending and receiving communication. Physical expressions of intimacy, and sexual intercourse itself, can be pure. So what *is* purity, exactly?

When we were first thinking about this question, we thought a lot about purity as a virtue – a habit we develop, with God's help, to become more the people God calls us to be. When purity is seen as the absence of physical intimacy, simply wearing a suit that would protect us from physical contact with other people would make us perfectly pure. Don't worry, though – since God calls us out of ourselves, into relationships with other people, and since the Church hasn't issued protective clothing, purity must be more than a lack of physical intimacy.

What does "purity" mean, anyway?

Purity is not the absence of physical intimacy! Purity is speaking the language of the body honestly and appropriately, with wonder and respect for the mystery and dignity of all human persons.

The most satisfying definition for purity we've found starts with the understanding that our bodies help us communicate with others. Pope John Paul II talked a lot about "the language of the body." Communicating physically is an essential part of human relationships. This means that when we are angry, tired, annoyed, happy, excited or in love, our bodies will play a healthy and important part in how we communicate with those around us. Purity can be defined as "speaking the language of the body honestly and appropriately." If we understand purity this way, then the question "How pure can we be?" still needs to take seriously the question we started with: "How far can we go?"

The "This Far!" Model

The "This far!" model, on the other hand, is very clear. If the line is drawn before "prolonged kissing," for example, then anyone who engages in prolonged kissing is going too far. The Church's hard line is "no sex before marriage." Neither we nor the Church think that this means that everything else is okay. What it does mean is that when someone gives you a hard line other than "no sex before marriage," it is advice, not Church teaching. We have heard all kinds of different hard lines for appropriate physical intimacy before marriage. Some people say only hold hands. Others say light kissing or hands above the waist and outside of clothing. Some people are told to keep both feet on the floor. These different lines lead to confusion. We may be tempted to choose the one that suits us. And, it's just plain ridiculous. We would laugh out loud if someone told us that dating couples could kiss for 3.4 seconds between two and five in the afternoon on weekends, with the lights on and both feet firmly planted on the floor.

We're being silly, but this silly example shows that there are major problems with this model. First, it assumes that every pair of non-married persons in a romantic relationship is at the same stage as every other pair. But acts that may be appropriate for some aren't always appropriate for others. Second, it presumes that everyone means exactly the same thing by terms like "prolonged kissing," and that everyone understands physical expressions of intimacy in the same way.

Everything but sex?

The Church does not have specific teaching on each possible act of physical intimacy. For example, the Church has made no pronouncements about the suitability of holding hands or French kissing for unmarried people. If it did so, Christian morality would be nothing more than strict legalism. Christian ethics aims to form people of virtue. Such virtuous people are able to discern how God calls them to act in given situations. The Church's official hard line on pre-marital intimacy is that Catholics should not have sex before marriage. This does not mean that everything else is fine; rather, the couple will need to discern what is right. Our model offers a way to help you discern how different expressions of physical intimacy may or may not suit your relationship.

Though the Church doesn't officially say more than "no sex before marriage," there are two things we want to mention. First, though some acts are fine for unmarried couples in principle, couples should not engage in them if they make avoiding sex a great burden. If anything you are doing with your partner puts you in a situation where sex seems inevitable, you should hold back. Which acts have this effect on you can change from person to person and circumstance to circumstance. Discernment in this area demands being honest with yourself and with your partner.

Second, there is a category of acts that mimic sex. These include oral sex and manual sex. In our presentations, we call them "mimicking acts." They deserve special attention here. A mimicking act is any act whose natural conclusion is orgasm. How do such acts fit within Catholic dating?

They don't. Their potential for orgasm means they can have many of the same implications as intercourse in a relationship. Sharing an orgasm with another person makes you feel incredibly close to them – spouse close. If you're not spouses, this intimacy is inappropriate.

It can be difficult to experience the fullness of marital intimacy with your spouse if you have routinely shared orgasms with other people with whom you did not have a permanent commitment. (We'll talk more about these activities in the context of marriage in Chapter 10.)

Imagine the following two couples. Jack and Jill are in Grade 9. They've known each other for less than a year and have been dating for less than a month. They really like each other and everything seems to be going well, but they both know that they are quite young and that they don't know all that much about the other person yet.

Mike and Mandy are young professionals in their mid-20s. They met at university and started dating in their second year. They have been together for over four years, and have been engaged for just over one year. They recently bought a house. Mandy will live in it until the wedding, then Mike will move in, too.

There is simply no way that all of the expressions of physical intimacy that are appropriate for one of these couples are appropriate to the other. Their situations are just too different.

Now, imagine that Jack and Jill are using the "This far!" model. They are told that anything beyond "light kissing" is for married people only. With this knowledge, they proceed to do everything that they think is less intimate than light kissing. This takes them about two weeks. Now, with the certain knowledge that they have to wait at least five years before they can possibly get married, they set about the task of not doing anything else for the next half-decade. We leave it to you to determine how likely they are to succeed.

Mike and Mandy, on the other hand, have been dating for five years and are engaged. Around two years into their relationship, they defined their kisses as "light." Several months later, after a major disagreement and the hard work that got them through it, they were much closer than they were before, and their kisses got a little deeper. They feel good about their physical intimacy, but they don't talk about this aspect of their relationship with other Catholics because some of their friends would say they've crossed the line. So they keep the discussion about physical intimacy entirely private.

At this point, the problem with the "This far!" model should be clear. It has no way of accounting for the differences in the situations of various couples, or for the fact that healthy relationships grow in intimacy over time. Jack and Jill are not Mike and Mandy. Jack and Jill's relationship in Grade 9 is not the same relationship they will have, if they are still together, when they graduate high school, or leave home, or get a job, or go to college or university, or get engaged.

The failures of these two models were the starting points we used to figure out a dating model for the young people at our first "sex talk."

We knew that we needed to find a way of answering the question "How far can we go?" that does the following things:

- does not imply that physical intimacy is impure,
- considers much more than just the physical aspect of relationships,
- takes into account that couples are in a great variety of different situations,
- acknowledges that healthy relationships grow in intimacy over time and, finally,
- gives practical answers for real couples in real relationships.

We think we've managed to do that. If you want to see what we came up with, you'll need to read the next chapter.

4

So, How Far Can We Go?

I f you're one of those people, like us, who finds the typical Christian answers (found in Chapter 3) to the question "How far can we go?" too vague or too unrealistic to work with, we hope the model we present in this chapter will help you. We do, however, need to start with a warning. This model presumes that those who use it are sincerely trying to live holy lives. If you're hoping to find loopholes so you can get away with as much as possible and still say you're following Catholic rules, this model isn't for you.

The most truthful answer to the question "How far can we go?" is simple: "It depends."

"Ha!" you say. "This silly book just finished criticizing people who give vague answers, and now they come at me with 'It depends.' How much more vague can you be? 'Depends' on what?"

Don't worry. The rest of this chapter deals with precisely that question.

If you've been living on Mars, or have just opened this book to this page, you may want to sit down before reading the next sentence. *The Church teaches that sex before marriage is wrong.* Yes, even if you really love each other. Yes, even if you're already engaged. Yes, even if humanity needed you to procreate right now to avoid the extermination of the human race. You thought the Church was all for procreation? Let us finish – just keep reading!

Imagine that you are stranded on an island in the middle of the Pacific. You have no reason to hope you will be rescued anytime soon.

You think you could survive for some time on the resources available on the island. The only other person there is a member of the opposite sex. You are not married to that person. There is no priest to marry you to that person. You are deeply in love with that person (and they with you). You want to commit your whole life to that person (and they to you). Can you have sex with that person?

From the previous paragraph you might guess "No." Actually, the Church's answer is "Yes!" How can this be?

The reason is *not* that in an extreme situation, it is okay to have sex without being married. The reason is that there is no reason not to get married. You are both deeply in love. You are willing to commit your whole lives to each another. You are prepared to accept children. As far as the Church is concerned, this is an ideal situation.

There is, of course, the small matter of the priest. While it is not okay to have sex before marriage in extreme situations, it *is* okay to get married without a priest in extreme situations. Why? Because the ministers of the sacrament of marriage are the couple themselves. The priest does not give you to one another: you give yourselves to one another.

So, how do you get married without a priest – or with one, for that matter? You promise to give yourself completely to the other person. Part of "completely," by the way, is "for as long as you both shall live." You are not giving yourself completely if you say, "I'll stay married to you for as long as I can stand to," or "Let's be married for as long as we're having sex," or "For as long as we both shall like."

The Church believes that marriage means giving one's whole self to another person and receiving that gift back from the other person. Marriage is a *whole self-gift*. You're probably getting used to this phrase by now.

Sex belongs in marriage because sex is nothing more, and nothing less, than the physical manifestation of the whole self-gift that is marriage. In fact, sex is so integral to marriage that if you and your spouse never have sex, that is reason for an annulment (recognition by the Church that a sacramental marriage never took place).

The Church says you can have sex with that other person on that island in the Pacific because sex is the physical way of showing that you have given your whole self to that person. With this point in mind, let's look a little closer at that phrase "It depends."

"How far can we go?

"It depends."

"Depends on what?"

"On how much of yourself you discern God is calling you to give to the other person."

It should be obvious by now why we said that this model presumes you are genuinely trying to live a holy life and are not looking for loopholes. Humans are good at deceiving themselves. It is easy for us to pretend we are answering the question "How much of myself does God want me to give to this other person?" when in reality we are answering the question "How much of this other person do I want to take for myself?"

If you are ready and willing (and called by God) to give your whole self to another person, fantastic! Have sex with them. Just get married first. If you or your partner is ready for sex but is not ready or called to get married, you need to look at why. For example, you might say, "We can't afford to get married yet. We want a big wedding with all our friends and family. We'll get married in a year or two, but we'll start having sex now, because we want to give ourselves to each other."

This attitude poses a problem. If money is the reason for not getting married now, you need to decide how much you want an expensive wedding. If a big wedding is that important to you, then wait. You're not ready to give yourselves to each other. If it's not that important, have a more economical wedding sooner.

Or, imagine *you* want to get married, but your boyfriend or girlfriend is not ready to make a lifetime commitment. You might be surprised how many young people who never planned on having sex before marriage get caught in this situation. It is very tempting to have sex just to keep the other person around until he or she is ready to commit.

If someone cannot commit their life to you, for whatever reason, sex is the one thing you shouldn't do. In fact, it usually makes things worse. It further separates sexual actions from the committed relationships we long for. Sex is not a shortcut to intimacy!

If you want to have sex but don't want to get married, you need to look at your reason for not getting married. If it's not a very good reason, work through it and then get married. If it's a good reason, then it's probably a good reason not to have sex. Sex speaks a profound language of the body that is both a sign and a source of the kind of unity that married people share. If you're not ready for marriage, then you're simply not ready for the demands of a relationship that includes sex.

If you understand our explanation of the Church's teaching on premarital sex, you should be able to follow our dating model. It works on exactly the same principle: physical gifts of self ought to reflect our self-giving in other areas of a relationship.

It is impossible to give a list of physical acts that correspond to how much you want to give of yourself. We don't give away measurable portions of ourselves with each physical expression of intimacy. It would be silly to say that holding hands is a gift of 5% of oneself, while open-mouth kisses give away 50%.

It makes no sense to think in terms of percentages, because that's not how love works! We love because God first loved us (John 4:19). God's love is limitless. It is multiplied when we receive God's love and offer it back to God and to others. Love is not a limited commodity that we must ration, for fear that we won't have enough to share with a spouse. As God's people, we constantly offer our whole selves to God through our service of and relationships within creation. The many small and truly loving gifts we offer to a person we are dating are offered as free gifts, for their own sake, without future strings attached. With every relationship we have, God communicates his love through us and in us.

Also, different acts mean different things in different cultures and to different people. For example, people may hold hands for a number of reasons: if they are afraid and are relying on one another for courage, if they are praying together, if one person is comforting the other, or if they wish to show affection.

Since the Church doesn't tell you what physical expressions are appropriate in every possible dating situation, we'd like to offer some advice. We hope it can help you to discern what God is asking of you in the many relationships you will have in your life, particularly your romantic ones.

So how do you discern all this? In Chapter 2, we said that a human person is both physical and spiritual. This unique combination means that we are also emotional, social and intellectual. To give a whole self-gift to another person means giving yourself physically, spiritually, emotionally, socially and intellectually. All of these parts are interconnected.

We already know what it means to give your whole self physically. What would it mean to give your whole self socially?

The fullest social gift is sharing a home with your spouse. (Sharing a house or apartment with a roommate or two is not the same, as there is no lifelong commitment to each other. Married couples who treat each other like roommates often find themselves in trouble: a marriage demands much more unity!)

Full social intimacy doesn't mean that you will always go to the same parties. But it does mean that your spouse knows what parties you are going to and accepts that you go to them.

Full social intimacy means being willing to meet each other's friends. It means that, unless there are abusive relationships in the family, you not only put up with but strive to enjoy each other's families. It means checking with your spouse before you make plans. It means searching out activities you can enjoy together. It means working through your problems even if giving up might seem easier. It means supporting each other's career choices. If you are blessed with children, it means raising them together, as a family. In short, full social intimacy looks a lot like a healthy marriage. Funny thing.

What about social intimacy when you are dating? At first, you may spend time as friends doing activities you enjoy, but you do not always need to let each other know if you're doing something else. Once you're officially a couple, you may check with your boyfriend or girlfriend before making plans for Friday night, but would not want him or her to make all your plans for the two of you. It would be okay to break up with your boyfriend if you can't stand the way he talks to his parents, but it would not be okay to leave your husband over it.

Just like physical intimacy, social intimacy should gradually increase as you get closer to marriage.

Take a minute to think about what some spiritual, intellectual and emotional self-gifts might look like. (Check out the boxes below for some of our ideas about these kinds of gifts.) Can you share your feelings with each other? Are you comfortable praying together? What are your views on life, money, school, careers, sex, kitchen cabinets, and other important things?

How might you give yourself emotionally, socially, spiritually, intellectually and physically? What gifts has God given you in each of these areas? In which areas might God be calling you to grow? The first stage of discerning in dating and marriage is learning about yourself. The more you know about yourself, the better prepared you are to make decisions about your relationships and your vocation.

As we developed our dating model, many people asked us what it would look like to grow in or share emotional, social, spiritual or intellectual intimacy. We have put together a few of our experiences in sharing different parts of ourselves. Think about what you might add to this list, and what these particular actions might communicate for you.

Actions that contribute to emotional intimacy

- Sharing laughter
- Sharing a secret
- Forgiving another person and being forgiven
- Grieving with/for another person
- Sharing tears
- Articulating your feelings honestly
- Working at understanding your emotions
- Encouraging someone
- Becoming more self-aware about your motivations

Actions that contribute to intellectual intimacy

- Sharing your interests with others
- Being open to a new idea and the person who shares it with you
- Having an open and respectful debate
- Carefully explaining your perspective in a disagreement
- Being humble enough to consider the possibility that you might be wrong
- Sharing your enthusiasm about the latest piece of trivia you learned
- Sharing your knowledge about a piece of art or music
- Appreciating another's gifts of brilliance
- Learning from others

Actions that contribute to social intimacy

- Listening to others speak about their lives
- Telling your stories with generosity and respect
- Introducing your friends to one another
- Finding joy in the company of another person
- Welcoming a guest to a family meal
- Receiving an invitation to share a meal with others
- Being hospitable
- Spending a Saturday serving a meal at a soup kitchen
- Offering to help someone who is struggling with a heavy suitcase
- Doing a chore that isn't your job
- Borrowing or wearing someone else's school jacket or favourite sweater
- Naming the type of relationship you have ("This is my boyfriend, Joe," sounds a lot different from "This is Joe, the guy who delivers our flyers.")
- Trusting others to respect you and your relationships when you are apart

Actions that contribute to spiritual intimacy

- Praying for yourself, for others and for the world
- Praying with others in private
- Attending Mass or a liturgy with others
- Sharing a prayer before a meal
- Offering your daily work to God as a prayer
- Learning about your spirituality
- Sharing your gifts of spirituality with others in an inviting and respectful way
- Enjoying the beauty of God's creation with others

Actions that contribute to physical intimacy

- Feeling comfortable around others
- Trusting your gut when you feel uncomfortable
- Being confident in your self-worth: you are created in the image of God!
- Talking about physical boundaries
- Thinking about what you want to communicate with your body
- Offering a handshake
- Offering a hug
- Offering a helping hand
- Caring for someone who is ill or elderly
- Respecting personal space
- Greeting a friend with a kiss on the cheek

You need to think about and recognize how these factors play out in relationships before you can answer the question "How far can we go?" Why? Because our emotional, social, intellectual and spiritual actions can help us to discern appropriate expressions of physical intimacy.

Imagine your relationships as a graph. The *y* (vertical) axis in Graph 1 represents the level of intimacy you have with the other person in the relationship. The *x* (horizontal) axis represents the amount of time you have spent with that person, and your level of commitment.

Graph 1

Intimacy

Time / Commitment

If you had never met someone, you could plot your position on the graph at the origin (where the two axes meet). You have no intimacy with that person and no time spent or commitment made. This is a stranger. Every person you know now (except perhaps your mother) was a stranger at some point.

This means your future spouse will have been a stranger at one point – you shared no intimacy and had no commitment. When they become your spouse, your commitment and intimacy reach a certain fullness. We have added two more lines to create Graph 2 to indicate fullness of commitment and fullness of intimacy.

Graph 2

Intimacy

Stranger

Spouse

Time / Commitment

The process of meeting, dating, becoming engaged and getting married is a journey from stranger to spouse; from no intimacy to spousal intimacy; from no commitment to marital commitment. We'll use this chart to help you navigate the journey from stranger to spouse in a holy and fulfilling way.

A graph representing physical intimacy in the "How pure can we be?" model might look like this:

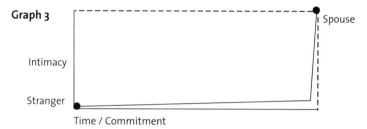

Physical intimacy is seen as impure and is basically avoided in the dating relationship.

A graph representing physical intimacy in the "This far!" model might look like this:

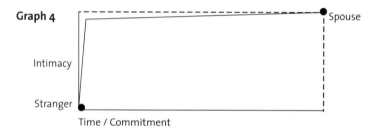

Couples do everything they can imagine that is less intimate than the particular hard line they have been advised not to cross. This probably takes a few weeks or months. Then they try to hold steady.

We all know that the shortest distance between two points is a straight line.

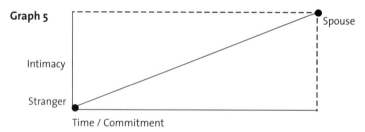

This is a good starting point. It shows that intimacy needs to grow gradually over time.

We think the straight line is better than Graphs 3 or 4, because it allows intimacy to grow as your commitment to your partner grows.

The straight line would be perfect if humans were perfect. If we could be sure that we always grew in intimacy as we spent time with someone and increased our commitment to them, then a steady progression of intimacy matching commitment would always be appropriate. The problem is we have trouble gauging our commitment and knowing how to match it with intimacy. Worse, sometimes we are selfish and try to take from our partner more than either of us is prepared to give. This can happen in any of the five areas of the human person that we discuss, but at this point, we are especially concerned with the physical aspect of human relationships.

So we think a better graph might look like this: a sloping line that starts slowly and increases only later. (See Graph 6.) It gives us room to discern carefully, and a bit of insurance if we are tempted to be selfish. We can choose to move forward in our physical intimacy with caution and respect, while acknowledging how important physical intimacy is. When we start things a little more slowly than might be necessary for perfect people, we move forward in the hope that the mistakes we make as imperfect people won't be nearly so hurtful for ourselves or for others.

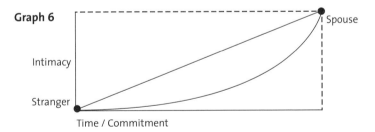

If your basic path starts lower, there is lots of room for getting to know each other and exploring physical intimacy together without crossing lines you don't want to cross.

The shaded area on Graph 7 is what we call "the safety zone." Intimacy progresses slowly as commitment grows, but there is room for mistakes. A healthy physical relationship should stay in this area.

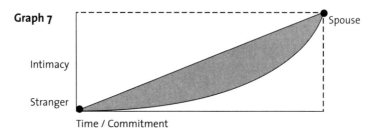

We start out far from marriage (on the bottom left of the graph). The farther you are from marriage in terms of time and commitment, the lower your physical intimacy should be on the scale. It should gradually increase as you get closer to marriage. But how can you tell if you're getting closer to marriage? All the other areas of intimacy in your relationship should be slowly growing as well. Remember the boxes we looked at that talked about different expressions of intimacy in all five of our categories? You should be able to discern a healthy growth in all of these areas. If any area is suffering, it will need work. It may even be a call to recognize that this particular relationship is not what God is calling you to at this time.

Assuming you are called to pursue the relationship further, you can use the other areas of intimacy to gauge appropriate expressions of physical intimacy. If you and your partner are progressing in a healthy way in your emotional, spiritual, intellectual and social intimacy, then it is natural and healthy to progress in your physical intimacy. If you are struggling in any of those areas, it is a sign to slow down physically.

Another thing to be aware of when making these decisions is the length of time before you might reasonably get married. If you can't possibly be married for another five years, that is a good reason to take things slowly: not just physically, but in every other aspect, too. If you are in a position where marriage is a genuine possibility in the next couple of years, your intimacy will naturally progress at a quicker pace. For this reason, high school students will naturally have relationships with much lower levels of physical intimacy than university students or people in the workforce.

A healthy relationship that is growing in all areas of intimacy should look something like this:

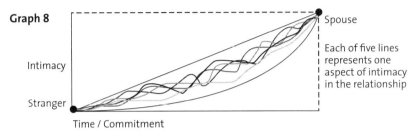

Why the slower growth at the beginning, with quicker development as marriage approaches? We've already mentioned that this approach can keep us from hurting one another when we make mistakes, but there is another reason. Our intimacy takes natural jumps at certain stages rather than showing perfect steady growth throughout the whole relationship. For instance, talking about getting married, or getting engaged, puts a relationship into new territory in terms of intimacy and commitment. This new level should be mirrored in a couple's physical (and emotional, spiritual, social and intellectual) intimacy. Working through a major disagreement often leads to deeper intimacy in a relationship. So might going through a traumatic experience together.

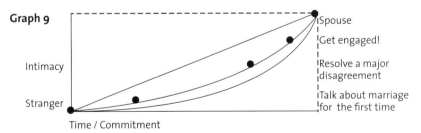

Here, then, is what a healthy relationship looks like. Intimacy grows over time and with commitment: slowly at first, to allow room for learning about each other. As a couple approaches marriage and the prospect of giving themselves fully to one another, intimacy grows to reflect the deepening reality of their relationship.

While we don't encourage "hard" lines, "soft" lines can help increase communication and set boundaries that respect both partners.

Most couples find it much easier not to "go too far" physically if they have had a serious and open discussion about what acts they think are or are not appropriate for their relationship at the time. Let's look at an example.

Greg and Valerie are college students who have been friends for a few months and have decided to start dating. At first they are shy about their physical intimacy, but as they become more comfortable with each other, things start to happen that were not planned. A kiss goodnight at Valerie's door ends up being a bit longer and more involved than either of them had anticipated. Greg was nervous about kissing Valerie. Valerie knew she wanted to kiss Greg, but wanted him to make the first move. When he did make the first move, they were both so excited that they didn't even consider how big of a kiss this first kiss should be. A long and intense kiss was not what either of them could honestly say reflected their commitment to each other at this point, but that's what happened.

Now, there is no need to panic here. A long kiss with both parties fully dressed and all four feet on the floor is not the end of the world. If, however, Greg and Valerie continue to engage in physical intimacy with no idea of each other's expectations and with no clear picture of how that intimacy is related to the rest of their relationship, it won't take long before they've both done something that could be much more damaging than a kiss that lasted a little too long.

This is where "soft" lines can help. Imagine that Greg and Valerie had been mature enough and clear-sighted enough to sit down and talk about their physical intimacy before engaging in it. They could have both said that they saw no problem with light kisses goodnight after dates at this stage, but that more intense kissing seemed not to reflect the reality of their current relationship with one another.

It would still have been romantic and exciting for Greg to build up the courage to plant that first kiss on the porch, but there would have been far less chance of going too far. Even if one person had a momentary lapse of self-control (and this happens to the best of us), the other person's saying, "Hold on, didn't we say we weren't going to do this yet?" can be just what is needed to get back on track.

If you're thinking that talking about physical intimacy seems a little awkward, think of the last time you were in a situation where both people expected some sign of physical intimacy, but no one knew quite how to move forward. Talk about awkward! Sometimes when someone makes the first move, we just go for it, not because we truly care about the other person, but because it's such a relief to finally get it over with!

Talking about physical intimacy may be awkward. But it's no more awkward than guessing your way through it with someone you *haven't* talked to about it. Being able to talk about physical intimacy is part of building healthy intimacy. If you don't feel comfortable talking with your partner about it, that is a strong sign that your physical intimacy should be at the low end of the scale.

Plus, talking about physical intimacy is great preparation for a happy marriage. All the experts will tell you that good communication between spouses is essential to great sex lives.

Let's imagine Greg and Valerie again. The morning after their first kiss, they both feel a little funny. Valerie calls Greg and says she'd like to talk about what happened. Greg is a little nervous, but he's also relieved, because he knew in his heart he needed to talk about it, too.

They meet for a walk in the park that afternoon. The conversation goes something like this:

Valerie: "I had a great time last night, and I'm really excited that you care enough for me to want to kiss me. I wanted to kiss you, too. It's just that what happened was a bit much for a first kiss. It seemed so intense."

Greg: "That's a relief. I'm happy you wanted to kiss me too. I am really enjoying getting to know you. I didn't plan on being so intense. I just got carried away in the moment."

Valerie: "Tell me about it!"

Greg: "So, does this mean no more kissing?"

Valerie: "No. I loved that you kissed me goodnight. It felt right ... at first. Then it got a little weird. It just means no more kissing like we did last night. At least, not right now."

Greg: "Okay. I think that is better, too ... at least until we get to know each other better."

Greg and Valerie have made a "soft" line. They know they won't kiss intensely – not because it's evil, but because it's not right for their current relationship. What about in the future, say, four months later? Let's see how they are doing...

In the last four months things have gone really well for Greg and Valerie. They have started going to church together on Sundays, and they pray together before meals. Greg went home with Valerie for a long weekend and met her family. He had a great time visiting her parents and siblings and hearing stories about Valerie when she was younger. Valerie has learned that Greg is good at listening to her when she comes out of class very excited about a new idea the professor explained. They've gotten to know each other's friends. If Greg goes to visit Valerie but she's not home yet, he chats with her roommates. They think he's great. Valerie has joined Greg and his buddies for a few poker nights.

They've also learned that neither of them is as perfect as they seemed at first. Sometimes Valerie overbooks herself and lets down people she had commitments to (including Greg). Sometimes Greg acts like he's got all the answers, without realizing how difficult someone else's situation might be. They've been able to recognize these faults in each other and talk about how they might work through them.

Do you see what's happening here? Greg and Valerie are slowly increasing their social, emotional, intellectual and spiritual intimacy. But what does their physical intimacy look like?

Well, they've been careful not to cross the line they set for themselves that afternoon in the park. Once in a while, a kiss goes a little longer than planned, but it usually breaks off with a laugh when someone realizes what's happening. Little kisses on the forehead or cheek are very common, and light kisses on the lips mark almost every time they meet and part. Valerie now feels very safe and secure when Greg stands with his arm around her waist, and Greg loves when Valerie tickles him by letting her lips touch his ear when she whispers to him.

They have been able to slowly grow in physical intimacy without crossing boundaries they have set together. They are getting more comfortable with one another's bodies, but neither Greg nor Valerie has ever felt used.

One day Greg says he thinks it's time to talk about moving the "soft" line up a bit. At this stage in the relationship, longer kissing might be appropriate. Valerie says she wants to kiss him and thinks it would reflect what is going on in the rest of their relationship. She adds that, if they are moving on, they need to set a new "soft" line so they don't get confused or hurt each other. Greg agrees.

When they do share a longer kiss, both Greg and Valerie are thrilled. It feels good and pure to share their affections that way. They know the kiss means that the other person cares about them deeply, not simply that they are feeling frisky.

This is how our dating model works. Couples slowly increase their physical intimacy to match the increase in intimacy in the rest of their relationship. The only way to be able to do this is through good communication. You have to know what you are willing to give of yourself in every aspect of your life. You have to talk with your partner about problems, and share your hopes and fears with them. Then physical intimacy is never an accident, but always a careful decision so that each partner knows how much the other cares for them.

What about spontaneity?

Does this approach to physical intimacy (or any other kind of intimacy) limit spontaneity in relationships? In *The Theology of the Body*, Pope John Paul II talks about freedom being more than just doing whatever we want. True freedom and spontaneity occur when we act in a way that is truly good without even thinking about it. That means that we develop virtue through good habits. If we hurt ourselves or one another by a spontaneous action, we are acting out of our sinfulness – and that's not a positive spontaneity. Practising virtuous actions, such as talking openly about physical intimacy and learning to be self-aware about why we do what we do, helps us to become people who are more likely to be spontaneously loving and holy.

Imagine that Greg and Valerie keep following this model, adjusting their expectations and limits every few months until they are married two years later. In that time, they will have learned to trust one another with their thoughts, their emotions and their bodies. They will have learned how to communicate affection. They will have grown spiritually in their relationship with God and with one another. In other words, they will have paid close attention to all the facets of their relationship. And they will know, on their wedding night, exactly what each person means when they offer themselves fully to the other when they make love. The thrill they felt at their first long kiss will pale in comparison.

5

Dating Is Discernment!

So now you have some idea of how our dating model works. While we were developing this model, we were both trying to figure out how dating should work. We did a lot of reading on the topic and talked to leaders in the Christian community whose advice we trusted. We think our model has several advantages over others we've seen.

• *This model takes your uniqueness into account.* God created only one person on earth who is just like you. Likewise, your parents, siblings, friends and potential boyfriends or girlfriends are perfectly unique. You may have noticed that our model does not give you a perfect age to start dating, a guide to finding the person who was made for you, or a map of which parts of the body can be touched at which times. There's a good reason for this: every person and every relationship is unique. Our model asks that you take responsibility for yourself and your relationships.

Take responsibility? Wouldn't it be easier if your parents, your friends, a set of rules or a book on sexuality made these decisions for you? Isn't being responsible for your own decisions dangerous, with the potential for you to mess things up royally?

Well … yes, it is a bit risky. But when God created the world, human persons were given freedom with an open invitation to love God. And humans have messed up royally, over and over again. But God gave us free will because you can't become a person of love if others make your decisions for you. And there is nothing more adventurous and exciting than being transformed into a person of love.

Our relationships with God and with one another do not come with a code of conduct to cover every possible situation. We each encounter God in different ways! Have you noticed that on any given Sunday, different Catholic churches have different styles of music, different traditions for their communities before and after Mass, and different programs going on during the week? Religious communities (such as the Jesuits, the Missionaries of Charity, the Grey Nuns and the Dominicans) have different ways of communicating God's love in the world and different styles of prayer. And yet, each community shows us one way we can enter into a life of relationship with God and one another.

• *This model is a guide for discerning relationships.* You have relationships with your parents, grandparents, siblings, teachers, friends and maybe someone who is more than a friend. As you choose to date someone, you start the process of asking yourself, your partner and God if this relationship might become a marriage. If the two of you are unique creations of God (and you are!), then this relationship will be different from any other relationship either of you will ever have. If you answer a call to marriage, you will move from stranger to spouse with one person. Although there can be no one-size-fits-all pattern for getting from stranger to spouse without any mistakes, our model can help guide you (and your future partner) to discern God's will in that experience. It is also important to note that this model suggests that dating is discernment about marriage. While you cannot know if you are called to marriage with a particular person until you discern together, you can know that a particular person is *not* someone you would be willing to marry – in which case you shouldn't date them at all!

What is discernment, anyway?

Discernment is living with the knowledge that God is always present, always active in our lives, even when God seems absent or silent. While the rarest few sane persons may actually hear God speaking to them, most of us have to find ways to make holy decisions by looking for God's voice in the people we meet and situations we face.

Discerning requires all the parts of us! We need to pay attention to our emotions and what they are telling us. We need to seek out accurate information to make good decisions. We need to listen to the wisdom of our bodies. Certainly, we need to be prayerful people. We also need to recognize that God is present in the community, and so our discernment must include conversations with people in the Church: parents, teachers, pastors and friends who will listen to our thoughts and help us to ask the right questions and make the best decisions.

Sometimes, because of the presence of sin in our world, we can mishear God. Discernment is not always a guarantee that we'll get it right, but it is a commitment to a process of seeking God and listening to hear God's wisdom in the advice of a teacher, in an experience of feeling that God is present to us, in the teaching of the Church, or in the nagging voice of our conscience. Luckily for us, God is merciful and keeps calling. As we grow into discerning people, we get better at listening to God and going back to him when we make mistakes.

Let's look at a few couples who are dating. How does our model fit for them?

Andy and Megan

Andy was 14 and Megan was 13 when they first met in the city-wide jazz band. They started dating about a year later, and played in the same band until they finished high school. From the beginning of their relationship, they both knew they wanted to study music at university. About two years into their relationship, Andy got his driver's license. All of a sudden they had more time to themselves, and their rare, quick goodnight kisses could be a lot more than rare or quick. One night, when they had kissed more than ever before, Megan stopped things and said to Andy, "I really like you and those kisses, but I'm feeling like things are going really fast. And I want to do much more than kiss you. But I'm 16. We've been saying we'll probably get married someday – but we both want to get university degrees before we get married. Besides, ever since you got your license, we haven't been seeing our families or friends as much. And they miss us as much as we're missing them." Andy had been looking out the window, but he turned to her and said, "You're right. If marriage is a long way off, we have lots of things to learn about each other before then, and we need to make sure we don't get carried away with the kissing. Cause I like it. A lot." Megan laughed.

Sarah and Peter

A lawyer who had just become a partner in her law firm, Sarah had spent many years focusing on her career. She had married during university. Shortly after her wedding, her husband died in a car accident. In the 12 years since his death, she lost herself in her work. In the past year, she finally went for counselling and went back to the sacrament of reconciliation to help her grieve the loss and work at healing some of her hurt. At 34, with a bit more time on her hands since she had earned her promotion, Sarah met Peter. Peter was 36. He had been working in Africa as a doctor and had recently returned home to take care of his aging parents. His years away had been mostly spent travelling. Each posting was for only a year, which made it difficult to have a relationship with someone. They met by accident one day when Sarah spilled her coffee all over Peter as she was reading the newspaper while they both happened to be sitting on a park bench. They ended up talking and quickly starting dating. After two months, they had met each other's families, realized that they shared a deep commitment to their common faith, and never ran out of things to talk about. One day, while they were having a quick lunch together before running back to work, Sarah looked at Peter and said, "Have you thought about getting married?" Peter, a bit shocked, said, "I've barely started kissing you, but yes, the thought has crossed my mind." They both left the restaurant grinning. Two months later, their families joined them at their parish to celebrate their wedding.

Joey and Tamara

Joey was 28 and working full-time at a sporting goods store. He met Tamara, who was 23, when she came in with her sister to buy a new bike. Tamara and her sister were planning an afternoon bike trip and invited Joey and a friend to come along. The four of them became friends. After a few months, Tamara and Joey decided to start dating. They had met each other's families and enjoyed each other's friends. Things were going well. Though Tamara wasn't Catholic, she respected

Joey's faith commitments and went to Mass with him when she could. After several months of dating, Tamara and Joey would hold hands and kiss briefly in public, and enjoyed cuddling and kissing when they were alone. Joey told Tamara he wasn't going to have sex before he was married. Tamara appreciated his honesty. She especially liked how he always told her what each touch between them was communicating. When Joey gave her hugs, he said, "Wrapping my arms around you is me saying that I love you *this* much!"

But, in time, Joey started to feel lonely when he was with Tamara. She always wanted to know if Joey loved her, but never said that she loved him. Though she was always respectful and interested in his faith, and was fantastic with his family and friends, she never really talked about any feelings or thoughts. When Joey brought this up one evening, Tamara went silent. "Are you afraid of telling me how you feel – about me, school, your family and friends?" asked Joey. Tamara looked at Joey and whispered, "I'm not afraid. I just don't know how." She burst into tears and told Joey that her family never hugged or touched and that they never talked about feelings growing up. "We have fun together," said Tamara, "but when I tried to tell them about being sad or excited, they told me to be quiet or they changed the subject. I like being with you because you tell me that stuff. But I don't know how to tell it to you." Joey smiled and said, "We need to work on this. I'm feeling really lonely when we're together because I feel like I don't know you." They talked some more. Tamara realized that she was in love with the idea of Joey, but she wasn't sure if she loved him for himself. At the end of their talk, Tamara said, "I think I need to figure this stuff out. Could we maybe take a break for a while? If we're going to be together, then I need to bring an emotionally healthy person to this relationship." Joey looked hurt, but replied, "Let's talk in a month. I want our relationship to be healthy, and if you being healthy means that we need to stop dating, I understand."

Our dating model can accommodate Andy and Megan, Sarah and Peter, and Joey and Tamara. Using the model doesn't guarantee that every dating relationship will end in marriage – and it shouldn't! But this model does help each couple to discern their spiritual, emotional, intellectual, social and physical intimacy, and to discover whether God is calling them to marriage or not. Marriage should serve both persons in the relationship, but the couple together will also be called to serve the community. Education, careers, community service and ideas about family all enter into the discussion. Couples in high school will need more time to figure out all that stuff. Couples that meet when they are already established in their communities have different challenges – such as finding the time to date and figuring out how two individual lives are going to blend into the shared life of marriage.

• *This model recognizes that growth in physical intimacy is a necessary and important part of relationships – including dating relationships.* The "How pure can we be?" and the "This far!" models presume that growth in physical intimacy happens in one or two giant leaps. Our model encourages couples to discover and talk about when their physical intimacy can move to another level. That is how our model makes you a better lover.

What?! How does this make you a better lover?

Let us tell you. When Brett was dating Flannery, for a very long time, she wasn't comfortable with kissing on the lips. Remember "soft" lines, from the last chapter? Out of respect for her comfort levels, and knowing that part of growing more comfortable physically is deepening emotional, spiritual, intellectual and social intimacy, Brett would kiss her on the cheeks, forehead, nose, eyes, chin, hands and ears. Sometimes, he would do this for an hour. Sometimes he kissed her in these places in the park, or on an elevator. For as long as it took for them to both be ready for the next step, Brett got creative about expressing his love for Flannery at the level of physical intimacy that she was ready for.

When you get married and start having sex, you will (we hope!) continue to grow closer to your spouse. Over time, you might want to express this really deep intimacy in a new way, by doing more with your spouse physically than you've ever done before. But, by then you're already having sex. You can have sex twice, or a hundred times, but you can't do more than have sex. So you have to learn to be creative in expressing your love through making love. If, while you were dating, like Brett and Flannery, you were growing in physical intimacy while respecting the comfort zones and the depth of your intimacy in other areas of your life, you might have learned 500 ways to kiss, touch or hold one another. That's the kind of creativity that will make you an amazing lover. Creative lovemaking will happen more easily for you.

You may have been told, as we were, that sexual experience with different partners will make a person's sex life better. But remember how we said that you are a unique person? Think of your friends or siblings. Are any of them exactly like you? A long "sex resumé" may mean that a person has had a lot of sex with other people, but this has nothing to do with his or her capacity to love *you*. Loving you is a unique skill. No amount of sex with anyone else will give your spouse the kind of experience that it takes to love you. When Leah and Marc were dating (though they had both dated other people), they spent three and a half years becoming lovers. They did not have sex before they got married, but Leah learned that Marc needed hugs when he was sad or angry, and that he liked to be touched gently. Marc learned that Leah needed to be touched when she was excited and happy, and that she hated it when he traced his fingers lightly over her skin. Marc is a fantastic Leah-lover, but his relationship with her does not make him skilled at loving every woman.

So, our dating model recognizes that you and each person you meet are individuals. It encourages gradual growth in physical intimacy and helps you prepare to be an attentive and creative lover. This dating model also helps you prepare for marriage in a few important ways.

• *This model is designed to help you see that your relationship has many areas that need to grow.* As you pay attention to how this relationship is significant emotionally, intellectually, socially and spiritually, and not just to the physical attraction, you are less likely to be blinded by "falling in love." Sometimes the high that comes from intense physical intimacy can make it hard for us to see what is going on in the rest of a relationship. We talk about this high as "falling in love," but such one-dimensional relationships aren't really love. Eventually, the couple realizes this, sometimes after much heartache.

• *This model allows you to balance your relationship so it can be healthy for both of you and be a place where you can serve your community together.* Because it requires you and your partner to talk about where you see successes in the relationship, and where you might need to do some work, this model teaches you that relationships can be hard work.

Two concrete problems when people "go too far"

Problem #1: The Invisible Couple

We've all been through this one. We are part of a group of friends, roughly half guys and half girls, that hang out together most of the time. Then, one day, two members of the group become an official couple, and all of a sudden they disappear from the face of the planet.

What is going on here? In most cases, they have let their physical intimacy get out of control, which damages the other four areas of their relationship. While appropriate physical intimacy enhances emotional, spiritual, intellectual and social intimacy, inappropriate physical intimacy hinders these other areas. In the above example, social intimacy is being hindered. The couple gets so overwhelmed with spending time together, doing things that you don't do when other people are around, that they stop making time to spend with their friends.

Teenagers know this is a problem. They even make fun of each other for it. So learn from it. Know when physical intimacy is throwing your social, emotional, intellectual or spiritual intimacy out of whack. Are you dating someone who isn't a very good listener when you want to talk about something interesting to you, but who is always up for a make-out session? Time to check your other areas of intimacy.

Problem #2: Unhealthy Relationships

Most of us know someone who has been caught in a bad relationship but just can't see it. Too often it is a girl who is being abused by her boyfriend. There are few things sadder than listening to someone make excuses for the person who is hurting them. Why do people put up with this? Usually they have gone too far, too fast. They have let the physical aspect of their relationship move way faster than the rest of it. Now they don't just have low emotional intimacy, they have negative emotional intimacy, but the problem is masked by the intense physical relationship. Controlling boyfriends or girlfriends might tell you not to see your friends, not to go to your church, not to talk to your parents. Sometimes they'll even make physical threats and carry them out. To avoid such situations, give yourself enough time to find out what kind of person you are with before things get out of control.

• *This model, when used properly, helps couples develop communication skills so they can talk about their relationship together.* Couples will recognize if they are incompatible in a certain area, or if it is not healthy for them to date. You may discover that God is not calling you and your partner to be spouses. This is part of what discerning marriage is about! Healthy sex lives (in addition to healthy domestic lives, and shared visions for careers and families) rely on the ability of spouses to speak openly and honestly about their feelings in relationships. This model helps dating couples to discern if marrying a particular person will help them to be the people God is calling them to be. It should help couples to see that relationships are built on mutual trust and honesty.

When Leah and Marc were dating, they got ahead of themselves in the growth of physical intimacy. They didn't have sex while they were dating, but in the first year, they went further than they were ready for. As you saw from the examples in the last box, physical intimacy that is more than what the relationship calls for usually ends up hindering the development of healthy intimacy in other areas. In her case, Leah started to feel intellectually and emotionally lonely in their relationship. They seemed not to talk anymore, and the only prayer they shared was at Mass on Sunday. You might think that this imbalance would have been obvious, but she felt so close to Marc physically that she couldn't see how the other areas of intimacy were being lost. Leah became so miserable that she broke up with Marc because she felt too disconnected by their lack of conversation. While they were apart, Leah and Marc both looked back over the relationship. They realized that they had been lazy about taking the time to talk, hang out with friends or pray together. They reconnected about a month later, with the shared goal of being more discerning about how physical intimacy should strengthen their emotional, spiritual, intellectual and social intimacy, rather than replacing all of these aspects.

Breaking up and our dating model

You are not called to marry every person you date. Dating is a process of discernment. Both partners are free to leave if they learn that they are not called to spend their life with the other person. Being too physically intimate can complicate the breakup process in at least two ways.

First, physical intimacy creates a strong bond that is difficult to ignore. The deeper the physical intimacy, the stronger the bond. If your physical intimacy is deeper than your commitment to the other person, it is hard to discern that God is not calling you to pursue the relationship.

Second, it can be difficult to stay apart after a breakup. Couples who know they have no future together can get caught up in an on-again, off-again cycle that is damaging to both of them. Couples that are used to a certain level of physical intimacy find it hard to give that up. Physical hookups trick the couple into thinking they can make things work. Once the initial high of the hookup has worn off, they can again see clearly that they don't belong together, so they break up. This can go on for months or years and cause serious emotional, social and spiritual damage. Plus it can prevent them from meeting other people who are much better suited to them.

Going separate ways

Before Brett married Flannery, he briefly dated a nice girl he met at work. Let's call her Sadie. (In other words, this is a true story, but we aren't using her real name.) They were both in their 20s. Brett had a lot of fun at work with Sadie. Eventually, they started seeing each other socially. Brett stopped by Sadie's other workplace to visit. Sadie took Brett as her date to a staff Christmas party. One night Brett made her dinner. Another night, they went dancing with some of Sadie's friends. The next day, Brett called and asked Sadie if she would like to go to Mass with him. She had grown up Catholic but wasn't in the habit of going to church every week. She was really touched by the invitation and happily agreed to join him. After Mass, Brett had to drop Sadie off at her other job. They were together in the car just outside the building, about to say goodbye, when Brett said, "I'm going to kiss you right now." Sadie looked at him. This would be their first kiss.

"But," he continued, "I want you to know what this means. I have really enjoyed getting to know you these last few weeks and I care about you a lot. I hope that you feel the same way and that we can continue getting to know each other in the future." Sadie was delighted. They kissed, briefly, and she went in to work.

Soon after, Sadie had the chance to go to Australia for a great adventure. It came up very quickly and she was gone in less than two weeks. It wasn't clear how long she would be away. Brett and Sadie both knew that their relationship was not yet at a point where they felt called to pursue it around the globe for an indefinite period of time. They parted as friends, hoping to see each other in the future.

By the time Sadie got back to Canada, Brett was engaged to Flannery. Sadie called him up and they went out for a walk and an ice cream. They talked about Australia and about Brett's being engaged. Brett had no bitterness that Sadie had taken her opportunity to travel, and Sadie had no bitterness that Brett was marrying another girl. They were able to have a perfectly comfortable relationship as friends, because their physical intimacy had never gone further than their relationship called for. They used it to communicate the truth to one another, not to use one another. Over ice cream, Sadie said, "You know, I tell my girlfriends that the kiss you gave me in your car that night was the best first kiss I ever had." Now, she wasn't talking about technique. Sadie felt valued that Brett was willing to tell her exactly what his actions meant. There was no concern that he might be trying to use her or see how far she would let him get. The link between the state of their relationship and their physical intimacy was clear. Because of that, they were able to go their separate ways when the situation called for it, with no hard feelings or confusion.

This dating model isn't a quick and easy fix for finding and keeping a spouse. It is a tool you can use to guide your relationship through some of the more difficult areas of discernment. Using this model in your relationships may help you to see that your vocation is to be single, for now or forever. Or, it can help you to prepare for a marriage that is emotionally satisfying, spiritually deep, intellectually stimulating, socially active and physically rich.

6

But Everyone Else Seems to Think It's Okay ...

As we said in Chapter 1, one of the reasons we felt we had to write this book is that a lot of people will tell you that the Catholic Church is against sex. Many good Catholics are convinced that because the Church is against artificial contraception, abortion, pre-marital sex, masturbation and other misuses of sexuality, the Church is against sex itself.

This is a bizarre way of interpreting the Church's stance on the issue of sex. Think of something you love – say, your favourite sport. You may love hockey, but that does not mean you love tripping, slashing, goaltender interference, cherry-picking, sucker-punching and hitting from behind. You know that there are penalties for those things in hockey because the game is better off without them. Hockey is more exciting, more safe and more satisfying when it is played with respect for the rules and the other players. Hockey is best when it is played the way it is intended. The same is true for sex.

There is one important difference to note here. The NHL, or what-ever body governs the hockey you happen to play, enforces penalties to ensure that the game is played the way it was meant to be played. The Catholic Church doesn't enforce penalties for people who go about sex all the wrong way. For one thing, the Church would have no way to go about enforcing penalties. The NHL can say, "You won't be playing hockey in this league anymore." But the Church can't say, "You won't be having sex anymore."

There is a better reason for the Church not to publicly enforce penalties on those who sin. God loves us and wants what is best for us, but gives us the gift of human freedom. The Church must communicate God's loving plan for us, respect our freedom and remind us that God offers us forgiveness when we go astray. Anyway, sin has its own built-in penalties: when we do things that aren't good for us, we hurt ourselves, we damage our relationships with others, and we damage our relationship with God. The Church wants people to have good sex because it knows that misusing sex can have powerfully destructive consequences.

What is sin, anyway?

Sin is not a list of fun activities that God or the Church forbids in a conspiracy to keep people from having a good time. Sinful behaviour does damage to us, to our relationships with others and to our relationship with God.

Think about a Ferrari. The people who build Ferraris write an owner's manual for the car. They tell you when to change the oil, what kind of fluids it needs, and how it works best. When you treat the Ferrari with respect and according to how it was created, it will have a long and healthy life. If you treat your Ferrari like a boat, however, you will run into major problems. Someone might try to convince you that taking the Ferrari for a sail might be fun, but it isn't going to go well in the long term.

We are all created in God's image, and we will have the best lives when we treat people according to their dignity. When we do sinful things, we do damage to ourselves and to one another. Luckily for us, God forgives and heals us when we make mistakes. But our best plan of action, and God's deepest desire for us, is to understand our true dignity and worth so we can avoid sin in the first place.

The Church does have some explicit rules regarding sexual activity. These have received quite a bit of airtime in Church documents and in the media. In this chapter, we will try to explain why the Church advises against pre-marital sex, promiscuity, cohabitation, masturbation and pornography. But we want to emphasize that these are not the only ways that we can hurt ourselves or others with our sexuality. When we choose the silent treatment instead of forgiving someone who has hurt us, we choose sinfulness. When we make bets about getting someone to date someone else, or blame our sinful thoughts on someone else's way of dressing, we fall into sin. We hope that the reasons we offer for the wisdom in these teachings will help you to avoid all kinds of sinful behaviours and attitudes.

Oh, and by the way, all of the topics we discuss here are relevant to both men and women. Often, the way sexual sins are presented gets them tied up with gender in confusing ways. Discussions on masturbation and pornography, for example, are almost exclusively aimed at young men. And young women are much more likely to be called nasty names for being promiscuous, or be given lectures about modesty. In our experience, this sort of classification is not only inaccurate, it is also damaging to both men and women. People of both sexes have struggled and do struggle with all kinds of sexual sin.

When considering sexuality and sinfulness, we must identify what makes a certain type of behaviour sinful. If sin damages our relationships with ourselves, others and God, then these activities are not just fun things that God or the Church wants to keep us from doing.

Learning to be a discerning person is often challenging. When we discover Church teachings that we disagree with or don't understand, we may be tempted not to listen. That way we do not have to be challenged or changed. The Church has been accused of having negative attitudes towards sexuality, or of being out of touch with reality because of its stance on some of these issues. When we encounter these sorts of sweeping statements, we need to take a closer look at why the Church continues to support these teachings. We must remain open to the possibility that the media has distorted these teachings or that we have misunderstood them.

Pre-marital Sex

Until recently in Western culture, pre-marital sex (sex before marriage) has been seen as a problem for one simple reason: it might produce a child, and that child would be at a serious disadvantage for not having been born into a stable home. Society's frequent rejection of both mother and child made matters even worse. Furthermore, someone would have to take responsibility for caring for the child if the biological parents were not able to do so. Before we had the technology to determine who the biological father was, a man could claim the child wasn't his. A woman was less likely to be working outside the home, or could get only lower-paying jobs, so it was hard for her to support a child on her own. Even now, when single parents receive much more support in our society, most will tell you that they wish they had the help and support of a truly loving partner to raise their children.

The widespread acceptance and availability of artificial contraceptives (and, when those fail, of abortion) has radically changed society's view towards pre-marital sex. In the name of liberating sex from negative attitudes and guilt, our culture wants us to believe that any sex is good anytime – and "safe sex" is society's solution to avoiding unwanted babies or diseases. Fostering healthy attitudes about sex, however, requires us to see that relationships, commitment, personal growth and even (perhaps especially) babies are part of the beauty and joy of sex. We should not wait to have sex in marriage because we are afraid of babies or diseases. We wait because we believe that sex is best when it works in and through us to express and build love between spouses who welcome and celebrate the consequences of sexual intimacy.

Most people who defend pre-marital sex describe it as a way for two people who love each other, or at least really care about each other, to express that love. Furthermore, many point out, marriage is often not feasible in the near future for some couples, and long-term celibacy can be a great burden. Many people cannot accept an outright ban on sex before marriage between two people who love each other. Such people are very often sincere Christians who have simply never heard a good reason for refraining from sex before marriage. Sometimes, young people are simply told that pre-marital sex is wrong, but not *why* it is wrong. Or people tell them to stay away from sex because it can lead to pregnancy and sexually transmitted infections (STIs). We think young people deserve a more thoughtful response.

Sex is a sign of married love; it is an expression of full commitment between two people. Unmarried people have not made a full commitment. Their love may be strong, and they may feel committed to the relationship, but genuine full commitment means a lifetime commitment. Such a commitment is not dependent on circumstances or emotions. That is why, when we marry, we promise to stay together "for better or for worse." If two people are in a position to make that promise, they should get married. Marriage is not something you do only after your student loans are paid off, your career is established, you have a house, you have done lots of traveling, and you have finished with the errors of youth! Marriage is about being called to share your whole life with another person.

There are many reasons why you might not be able to make such a promise. Here are a few, though you might think of lots more:

- Maybe you don't yet know yourself well enough to know if you can make or keep such a commitment.

- Maybe you have personal issues that you need to work through.

- Maybe (and very often this is the case) you just need to spend more time discerning if you are called to marry your partner.

Now here is the issue: any good reason why you are unable to promise your life to someone is a good reason not to have sex with that someone. Let's compare with the list of reasons above:

- before having sex with someone, you should know yourself well enough to be able to give yourself;

- you shouldn't enter into a sexual relationship when you have serious outstanding personal problems that you need to work out; and

- you need to be sure that you can enter into loving the other person fully and completely.

Furthermore, if you do have sex with someone and you don't know yourself, you have serious personal issues, and/or you aren't committed in your love for them, sex can further complicate the relationship and make it difficult for you to get out of the relationship.

Sex is a powerful gift. A couple discerning marriage needs to learn enough about themselves and each other to determine if they want (and are able) to promise their lives to one another. Pre-marital sex makes this task extremely difficult. Why?

If a couple that is discerning marriage has sex, they feel much closer than before. It becomes very easy to look past the other aspects of the relationship that might need work. It might even cause them to overlook the fact that they are not called to marry each other at all. Sex can make people feel as if they are in a fully committed relationship, even when they're not. They may make commitments based on the false intensity their relationship achieved because they had sex too soon. Many such relationships end with one partner saying, "I just don't love you anymore." Perhaps the problem is that they weren't able to be sure if they loved each other in the first place.

Not having sex before marriage can be very difficult. The media and popular culture try to convince us that everyone is doing it. In our society, we often prolong the time between sexual maturity and marriage by a decade or more. If you meet your spouse in your teens, waiting can be particularly challenging. But this challenge, if it is handled properly, can be a fantastic foundation for a marriage. A couple that refrains from sex until they have fully promised themselves to one another has several advantages. They can be confident that they discerned marriage without the overwhelming impact that sex can have on that decision. They can be confident that their relationship will survive if, for some reason, they can't have sex at some point. They can be confident that, should one or the other of them ever develop feelings for someone else (which is not so rare), they have the self-control not to act on those feelings. Not having sex can be a great sacrifice. Great sacrifices only make sense with great rewards. Here's the interesting thing about waiting to have sex until you're married: knowing that your spouse is willing to sacrifice for you is its own reward. It allows you to enter marriage freely, and it builds the level of trust that a wife and husband need to truly give of themselves and receive each other.

Pre-marital sex is not wrong because sex is bad or because being married is superior to being single. The Church advises us against pre-marital sex because sex speaks a powerful language of commitment and self-giving that is appropriate for people who have a married level of commitment to one another. Pre-marital sex is not a good idea because we speak a lie with the language of our bodies when we offer sex to another without freely offering the rest of ourselves and our lives to that person. Couples who wait until they are married to have sex are not promised perfect marriages or perfect sex lives, but they are building a foundation of trust and discernment in their marriage that will serve them well as they live out their commitment for the rest of their lives.

Promiscuity

In some circles, especially certain areas of pop culture, promiscuity is treated as a virtue, but most people do not really value it. Donna Freitas, in her recent book *Sex and the Soul,* concluded that most young people on American college campuses secretly prefer the idea of dating and romance to "hooking up," but often feel like they're alone in this. When we find ourselves immersed in a social setting where everyone seems to be offering physical intimacy separate from relationships, we may think we have to behave this way to be accepted. We might also be tempted to believe that our value as people is connected to our willingness to offer ourselves physically to others.

Rejecting this idea does not mean that we think sex itself is bad! Remember that a person is more than just a body. We are also emotional, social, spiritual and intellectual beings. Imagine what happens when we try to disconnect our physical selves (or, to reduce it even further, just our sexual selves) from the rest of our person. We cannot do it, but even trying to do it hurts us.

Imagine that Sue and David meet at a party one night. They've seen each other around but have never been introduced. Though neither of them has ever had a drink before, tonight they've both had a couple. They end up hanging out in the backyard alone, just talking at first. They've both kissed other people before, but always people they had been dating. All of a sudden, Sue decides she'd really like to kiss someone tonight. So she kisses David. David isn't opposed to the idea. Pretty soon, things have gotten out of hand. The next morning, Sue wakes up and can't remember what followed the kissing. She feels a bit guilty and dirty, but she can't explain why. She's worried about what her friends will think (or if they even know). And when she jumps in the shower, she can't help but hope that David will call her and want to go on a real date. Though she can't say this out loud, Sue's emotional self wants to be closer to this guy she's been so close to physically. Her spirit longs to be received alongside her physical self. She wants to be recognized socially as a girl who is valuable enough to be loved publicly. On top of that, her head is rationalizing last night's behaviour, telling the story as if what happened was perfectly all right.

Meanwhile, David wakes up on a couch in a room filled with his sleeping buddies. He remembers everything that happened the night before, especially the part after he told Sue that they'd gone too far, given her a hug and sent her home in a cab. Then he walked back into the party house, only to discover that three of his buddies had been watching him out the window the whole time. And then they started congratulating him. He was an instant hero. As he lies awake the next morning in the silence, he feels empty. Sue is a really nice girl. He'd really like to get to know her better, but she'll never want to talk to him now that everyone knows they hooked up. His head is telling him that guys aren't supposed to feel bad about this stuff – all his friends think it's just fine. And yet, he feels guilty and he can't really explain why.

David and Sue, with courage and grace and mercy, might meet again and become friends or decide to pursue a dating relationship. But they might feel too ashamed to seek forgiveness from each other. They might tell themselves that this is normal – until they actually believe it and do it again with someone else. They might convince themselves that they did nothing wrong. And until they seek out forgiveness and deal with the damage they have done to themselves and one another, they will carry around the negative baggage from that experience.

People have multiple uncommitted sexual experiences for many complex reasons. When promiscuity becomes a habit, it is easy to detach sex from the rest of what it means to be a person. We might be tempted to believe that any sexual experience is "good practice" for any other. Not surprisingly, having sex that is not connected to your personhood or the personhood of your partner makes it more and more difficult to feel unique and loved yourself. Feelings of emptiness can be at the root of promiscuity in the first place. Looking for love and ac-ceptance in casual sex can become a vicious cycle. It can end in terrible ways: strings of broken relationships, addictions and, perhaps worst of all, the inability to truly give yourself to another person. Promiscuity can severely damage the ability to give and receive gifts of self that are so necessary for fulfilling human relationships.

Cohabitation (Living Together Before Marriage)

Living together before marriage is so common now that it often goes unquestioned. The reasoning seems obvious enough: it is best to learn if you can live with someone before committing your whole life to them. What if you get married and then find out that you can't stand to live together? You're in for either a quick divorce, a life of misery, or some combination of the two.

A few years ago, a study came out that shocked a lot of people. It showed that couples that live together before they get married have a 60% *higher* chance of divorce than couples who wait until after the wedding to move in together. According to the study, living together without marriage was really bad for relationships.

How on earth could the divorce rate be that much higher for people who had done the "smart" thing and made sure they could live with their partner before tying the knot? (Now, some people have suggested that religious people are the ones not living together before marriage, and that these same people avoid divorce for religious reasons. They don't have better marriages, these people say, they are just more willing to stay in bad ones. The problem with this argument is that religious people have a divorce rate that is about the same as everyone else in the society. And, in any case, you would still need to show that religious marriages were more likely to be unhappy marriages, which hasn't been done.)

Many people justify living together by suggesting that we don't buy cars without test driving them first. Would car owners who test drove their vehicles before buying them have a 60% rate of dissatisfaction with their purchase? Of course not.

The answer to this riddle can be summed up in three simple words: PEOPLE AREN'T CARS! The Church believes that you should love people and use things, not the other way around. When you start loving your car like it's a person, you've got problems. Same thing if you treat your partner like a car.

When a car gets old, you trade it in for a newer one. When a car breaks down, you replace the parts or get rid of the car. If you come into some money, you trade your economical car for a more luxurious model. You can have two cars (or five, or ten). You do not expect the car you drive right now to be the one you'll be driving when you turn 85. When your car is acting stupid, you can hit it with a wrench.

You get the point.

Now, we're not saying that everyone who lives together before marriage is going to have a miserable relationship or end up divorced. We are saying that if we train our brains to think of our partner as some sort of commodity to be tested, we shouldn't be surprised if sometimes we start treating him or her like a commodity.

People who think they need to live together before marriage to find out if they can deal with being married to their partner are saying, consciously or not, "I think I love you, but I won't be sure if it's real until I know if you put the cap back on the toothpaste, and put the toilet seat down, and put my CDs back in their cases, and don't use metal in my non-stick pots and pans, and don't steal the covers, and do your share of the housework."

They have decided that their love depends on things that have nothing to do with love at all. They are saying, in effect, "I'm not sure if I love you enough to get married." And, if you don't know for sure if you love someone, the one thing you should *not* do is move in with them.

Moving in together is to social intimacy what sexual intercourse is to physical intimacy. To share a home, a kitchen, a bathroom and a bed is to be as socially intimate as it gets. It's not like having a roommate who comes and goes as he or she pleases. If you live together with a partner, you must plan your schedule around the other person. Your friends will have to start taking your partner's plans into account when they ask about your plans on Friday night. Your finances will be more dependent on each other than when you lived apart.

You are acting as if you have the fullness of commitment, but, in fact, your commitment is tending away from full commitment. Your actions say, my commitment is dependent on your moods, your problems, your behaviour.

A marriage commitment says for better or worse, in sickness and in health, in good times and in bad. A marriage commitment says, "as long as we both shall live." A relationship that needs a test drive says, "as long as we both shall like."

Imagine that your partner passes the test. You both decide you can live together. Their bad habits don't bug you as much as they might ….

Fine. You live together now. But what if things change? What if a medical condition makes a person unable to help around the house? To earn a living? To perform sexually?

A relationship that begins with a test drive at the beginning may well revert to that state if things get difficult. On the other hand, a relationship that says, "I love you so much that I am willing to work through any problems that may arise in the complications of sharing a home," also says, "I love you so much that I am willing to work through any problems that may arise in the course of our life together." Love that is dependent on circumstances that could change at any moment is not really love at all.

Marriage is a social ritual that confirms and celebrates the commitment between two people. This ritual helps us through the transition from two individuals into one flesh, and prepares us for the adventure of a lifetime together. The shared experience of publicly professing our commitment to one another can be a reminder of our promises and our desire to keep them.

Marriage is also a symbol of God's love for us. God has chosen to love us regardless of our weakness. Richard Gaillardetz says that marriage is "a daring promise"! We commit ourselves to the unknown, to an adventure with another person. Even when our circumstances change, God's love remains constant. The human heart craves this constant love. Marriages are challenging because we are sinful people – but the willingness to make and live a daring promise is a sign of hope that God is faithful.

Imagine how insecure you would feel knowing that your partner's love for you was dependent on feelings and circumstances, things that can change in an instant. Now imagine how secure you would feel knowing that, no matter what happens in life, your partner will stand by you, will *choose* to love you.

This is what we promise in marriage – to choose to love the other person every single day. This doesn't mean we'll never be angry with them. This doesn't mean we won't screw things up by hurting each other over and over again. It means that we receive God's gift of a love that is strong enough to deal with those things.

If marriages become abusive

The Catholic Church does not expect either spouse to stay in a situation that is abusive. Someone may be forced to leave for reasons of physical and emotional safety. This does not mean, however, that they stop choosing to love their spouse. Further, if the behaviour is corrected and the home is safe for both spouses and their children, reconciliation should be attempted. Where reconciliation is not possible, the separation will have to be permanent. Catholic marriage tribunals offer a ministry of reconciliation to couples whose separation has become permanent. In cases where, for a multitude of reasons, one or both spouses did not understand the commitment they were promising or did not fully commit to marriage, annulments of marriage acknowledge that the marriage was not truly or freely promised in the first place. Not all separated or divorced people choose to pursue an annulment, however. Some people choose to honour their lifelong marriage vows by living a loving single life after a separation or divorce.

Masturbation

The Church understands sexuality as a gift from God that draws us into relationship with other people. Fr. Ron Rolheiser, in *The Holy Longing,* describes sexuality as a fire or energy inside us that makes us delight in life and brings us joy in relationships. He reminds us that sexuality is much larger than having sex. In marriage, sex is one way we share the beauty of life with a spouse, but marriage is about a shared life, offered generously to one another and to the world. This works not simply because we are sharing a pleasurable activity. Sexuality draws us into communion with another person specifically by drawing us out of ourselves. Our sexuality exhibits a shared love, a shared joy, and a shared concern for the good of others.

All physical actions speak a language of the body, communicating our values and understandings in action. The problem with masturbation is that it says my sexuality is about me! When sexuality turns inward and focuses on my satisfaction alone, I stop thinking of others first. Our sexual activity, even more than our other actions, ought to draw us into deep and selfless relationships, for that is where we will find the deepest fulfillment in our lives.

Human persons long for communion with one another. We want to be acknowledged as valuable, loved and cared for. Masturbation reduces our sexuality to the pleasure of an orgasm, but orgasms by themselves cannot bring us into communion. When we masturbate, we miss out on the fully personal and relational gift of our sexuality. Masturbation teaches us how to feel (temporarily) satisfied, but what we need to learn is how to make our partner feel satisfied. Masturbation teaches us that sexual desire is healthy and normal, but it doesn't teach us how to pursue those desires in a way that is meaningful and life-giving.

Teenagers are often told that masturbation is a healthy way to sexual self-discovery, or that masturbation is better than pre-marital sex or promiscuous behaviour. But encouraging masturbation as a strategy to avoid pre-marital sex is bound to fail. Lack of self-control in one area is likely to result in lack of self-control in another area. Teens with enough self-control to avoid masturbation are actually more likely to resist hook-ups at parties, not less likely.

Women who have difficulty achieving orgasm during sex are often advised to masturbate to learn how to help their bodies get pleasure from sex. Yet, in an expression of patience, generosity and selflessness, spouses can explore this process together so both partners find greater satisfaction and fulfillment in their sexual life. The benefits of this approach can strengthen their intimacy in their sex lives and beyond.

Our sexuality is a gift, offered to us to allow us to find our joy in human relationships. When we use sexual action selfishly, we create habits and attitudes that make it much more difficult to allow sexual activity to nourish our relationships, to be a sign and source of unity and blessing from God.

The value of self-possession underlies this whole discussion. Self-possessed people act with true freedom: they freely choose to do what is right and good, knowing that this approach is best for them. They are not tossed about by temporary desires and impulses. They are capable of making difficult decisions and resolutely carrying them out. Self-possession is a gift from God, a virtue that we receive and develop with practice. Our consumer culture does not like self-possessed people. Our culture is organized around selling things to people. To sell things to people, we rely precisely on their lack of self-possession. People see an ad for ice cream, then suddenly they need an ice cream, whether it's good for them or not. The widespread acceptance of masturbation should not be surprising in a consumer culture where we are always encouraged to satisfy ourselves immediately. As followers of Christ, we are invited to live a counter-cultural witness that we are abundantly blessed, not that we need to be immediately gratified to be happy.

Before we know whether or not we are called to marriage, we are exploring relationships. The best preparation for single life, religious life or married life is developing healthy relationships and fostering virtues that make us more like Jesus. Long before we are sexually active, we can be developing joy in relationships and practising virtues that will make us generous and selfless people, whether we are married, single, or in religious life.

Pornography

Porn is available to anyone who can click a mouse. Even though more and more people openly admit to using porn, most still find it offensive, something they wouldn't want to admit to using. What exactly is the problem with pornography? Why are people better off without it?

Pornography removes human relationships from sexuality. It reduces the person in the image to what is sexually useful for the viewer. Because it involves no real relationships, porn can become a replacement for real relationships. It is very easy these days to live one's social life "virtually." Rather than heading out into the real world and meeting and engaging with real people, we use our computers, cellphones and Facebook profiles. This technology is not evil in itself, but it should enhance, not replace, real human contact. Porn reduces sexual intimacy to one's own demand, rather than being a process of discernment and discovery with someone you love.

The pornography industry creates a culture of exploitation (particularly of women) that markets and sells people as sexual objects. Morally, this is unacceptable. As Christians, we believe that all people are made in the image of God, and therefore deserve to be treated with dignity.

Pope John Paul II once said that the problem with pornography is not that it shows too much, but that it shows too little. What did he mean by this?

He was saying that porn shows only one superficial (often airbrushed or surgically altered) dimension of a person. It doesn't allow the people involved an opportunity to be fulfilled in relationship. The actress on the screen might love her cat and play the clarinet and visit her grandmother in the hospital each week, but we don't learn anything about that. There is no relationship. We find fulfillment when we belong to a community where we feel accepted, challenged and valued. No virtual reality will be able to provide us with the depth of relationships available in the people around us.

It shouldn't be a surprise that, since pornography separates sexuality from relationships, porn is bad for marriages. On top of encouraging a depersonalized view of sex, porn can hurt marriages by raising ridiculous expectations for how sex actually happens. Sex isn't supposed to be staged or professional. The best sex doesn't happen "like in the movies." Images, books, ideas or attitudes that reduce any person to a sexual object damage our ability to relate in a healthy way to real people.

Maybe you haven't ever used or been tempted to use porn. But the sin of objectification that lies at the heart of pornography happens in other ways, too. Have you ever heard a group of girls (or guys) talking about a particularly good-looking member of the opposite sex? Maybe the discussion is all about a girl's breasts or a guy's muscles. Maybe a girl meets a cute guy and decides they'll be married, have three kids and drive a minivan before she even learns the guy's last name. Like pornography, this kind of fantasizing reduces a person (in this example, a guy) to what is useful or desirable to the person doing the looking.

What about his thoughts on the matter? Maybe that guy is called to single life and to serve the world as professor of philosophy. Or maybe he wants fifteen kids and a motorcycle!

We are called to meet and experience others as whole people, as being created in God's image. Anytime we reduce a person to less than this, we are hurting our relationships with ourselves, with others and with God.

Conclusion

In this chapter, we haven't covered every possible misuse of relationships or sexuality. We haven't clearly and systematically refuted every argument that has been offered to support these behaviours. But we hope we have helped you understand that the Church's position is based on an understanding of just how valuable people are in God's eyes.

We should be able to enter freely and deeply into relationships, trusting that others are also respecting human dignity. Our bodies are not objects; they are the expression of our whole personhood. Our sexuality is a gift from God that calls us out of ourselves and into relationship with other people. When sexual activity is separated from the joy of relationship, we lose something important. When we separate orgasms from communion with a spouse, we lose depth of experience and meaning in marital sexuality.

Men and women of all ages who struggle with sexual sin (that is, most of us!) are trying desperately to realize our human dignity. We all have a responsibility to ensure that people are always treated as *whole* people. The dignity and intrinsic value of each and every human person is at the heart of our understanding of sexuality. Our longing for fulfillment in relationships will move us naturally into care and concern for all people. Whether we are called to marriage or single life, religious life or the priesthood, a healthy sexuality will move us to compassion for all people. When we understand our sexuality as the foundation for a healthy human community, we can start to see how our vocation (marriage or otherwise) is a gift to the world!

7

If You Have Already Gone "Too Far"

In reading this book, you may have become more aware of some ways you have been hurt by decisions you have made about sexual activity, or by the way others have treated you. In our friendships, dating relationships and marriages, we have made mistakes, too – causing pain for ourselves and for those we love.

Many of us have hard and painful stories relating to our sexuality. On the surface, some of these seem unrelated to sexuality – things like bullying or manipulation by people we thought we could trust – but our sexuality is involved whenever we are called into relationship. These kinds of harmful behaviours have a major impact on our ability to have healthy relationships. Painful breakups, pornography, masturbation, unexpected pregnancies, abortion, rape or sexual abuse have serious effects as well.

In some cases, we have been the victims of other people's sins. We are not to blame for those sins, but we cannot be healthy again unless we heal. If you get injured in a basketball game because someone else broke the rules, you have to take a game or two off to fix your ankle. The same is true of matters relating to sex. Asking for help is a key part of dealing with verbal, physical or sexual abuse, rape and abortion. Your parents, teachers, coaches, priest and counsellor can help you deal with these situations. This book is not a substitute for finding help to heal after any painful experience. Talk to an adult you can trust. Though it may seem like a sign of weakness, asking for help is a sign of growth and maturity. Part of being a Christian is being willing to depend on God. God gives gifts of counselling, healing, honesty, trustworthiness and healthy relationships to many people in our communities. Trusting in the gifts God gives other people is part of placing your trust in God.

In other cases, our own sin is at the heart of the problem. When we have been cruel to others, have avoided help for addictions or have chosen to be angry instead of to forgive, part of our healing is taking responsibility for our sin. Our God is a God of justice who respects our freedom. God allows us to experience the consequences of both our good and our not-so-good actions. But our God is also a God of mercy, forgiveness and love. No matter how many times we mess up, God calls us to return to him.

In the story of the prodigal son in Luke 15, Jesus tells of a son who has embarrassed himself and his family. Far from home, with no money and painfully aware of how badly he has messed up, the son decides to return home, even to work as a slave there. The son has done many things wrong, but his father, with great love and thankfulness, sees only his beloved son returning home. Sometimes asking for forgiveness involves going to someone who sees only our fault. But when we turn to God, expressing our sorrow and our desire to choose God, God accepts our apology, helps us to become better people, and loves us more deeply than we can know. Becoming aware of the depth and power of God's love for us will likely take a lifetime, but each time we return to God, we taste and see a bit more of God's love.

The sacrament of reconciliation is a key part of this healing process. Whether we are finding it difficult to forgive someone who has hurt us, struggling with an addictive habit, or wishing we could forgive ourselves for something we have done, reconciliation matters. When we sit with a priest for the sacrament, we confess our sin to God in the presence of a member of the community who represents the person of Jesus and who has been called to be the face of God's love. "Reconciliation" means to make peace. The sacrament allows us to make peace with God and to offer ourselves in humility to God's service within the community, which shares our commitment to loving God and one another. The priest welcomes us, reminds us that God rejoices when we return to him, shares our mourning over sin, and then celebrates with us the joy of being made clean.

To whom shall we go?

In John 6, as Jesus is teaching about what it means to follow him, people start to leave. The disciples get worried and say to Jesus, "People are leaving. This teaching is difficult." Jesus replies, "Do you also want to leave?" And Peter says, "Lord, to whom shall we go? You have the words of everlasting life."

The call to holiness can be intimidating, especially when we have made mistakes. Perhaps you're not sure if you've made mistakes, but you're afraid that, when it comes to purity and chastity, you will. Maybe you think you've messed up so badly that God could never forgive you.

Even when we hear the voice of Jesus, we remain free to say that we want to leave, to stop listening or to walk away. Jesus came "so that we might have life, and have it abundantly." If we leave him, where can we go? Our God has the words that lead to everlasting life. No matter how badly we've messed up, God calls us back to him.

Though God forgives us whenever we ask, the sacrament is a place where the grace of forgiveness meets us in relationship. You may or may not have noticed that all the sacraments are encounters with people. When we are baptized and confirmed, the priest or bishop blesses us and the community welcomes us into the Church in a new way. When people are married or ordained to the priesthood, the sacraments introduce new relationships. When we receive the Eucharist, we meet the person of Jesus, given for and shared by all members of the Church. In the same way, the sacraments of reconciliation and the anointing of the sick are occasions where we experience God through meeting another person.

With sexual sin, confessing can be especially embarrassing and hard. But, since our sexuality is about much more than just sexual intercourse, our sins in relationship with all people are especially important to confess and to heal. Our relationships with our families, friends and even our enemies will be much healthier and holier when we take our mistakes in relationships seriously and work hard to be people who communicate God's love to others.

No matter what we have done wrong, God's deepest desire for us is a life of great joy. The sacrament of reconciliation does not change what we have done in the past, but it helps us recognize that we have made choices that have stopped us from experiencing all the joy God intends for us. In the presence of someone who shares our faith, we turn back towards God. We put our trust in God's love. In the sacrament, God does what we cannot do: God recreates us, transforms our hearts and makes us new.

Being God's compassionate people

God has great compassion for us when we make mistakes. Most often, we experience this compassion through God's people in our lives who offer us reconciliation, forgiveness and love. Likewise, we learn to doubt God's compassion when God's people are people of judgment, cruelty or rejection.

When people we know make mistakes, we have an important role to play in their experience of God's compassion. This doesn't mean that we have to agree with everything that everyone does, but it does mean that we extend God's love to them through compassion and support in difficult times. For example, Catholic women have unplanned pregnancies just as non-Catholics do. As a community, our reconciliation with and support for a mother who faces an unplanned pregnancy can have a huge impact on her life and the life (or death) of her child.

God always offers us the chance to make things right through a forgiveness that calls us into a deeper relationship with him and with others. When you meet people who have made mistakes, or when you are tempted to refuse God's forgiveness for yourself, try to remember God's compassion. God longs to make things right in and through his people – including you!

God is calling you – and every person he created – into a life of love. To be invited into the love and life of God is to participate in heaven on earth. This does not mean that life will be easy or that we will have all kinds of material blessings, but it does mean that we will be increasingly aware of the presence of God in all aspects of our lives. As we work with God at becoming the people he created us to be, we become people who desire to be healed from the consequences of our own sin and the sin of others. We become people who desire and rejoice in virtue. And we become people who long to give love to others as God gives his own love.

8

So, You Think You Might Be Called to Marriage ⑨

We all come to a place where we are called to make a more permanent decision about our vocation. Single life, religious life and married life are three different ways of living out the gifts of our sexuality. At some point in a dating relationship, you may start to wonder if you are being called to let go of single life and embrace the adventure of marriage.

When we are single, we must discern whether this vocation is temporary or permanent. By focusing on the gifts we can offer to the world as single persons, we grow into a mature sexuality that will serve us and the world well in any vocation.

How do you know if you're called to marriage? First, though you might have a great desire to be married and to be a parent, marriage can be discerned only with your partner. Healthy, holy dating will move you into discernment of marriage in good time. But some key experiences can help confirm that your desire to ask the question about marriage might in fact be God's call to you.

First, you will notice that this relationship makes you a better person. Your future spouse should bring out the best in you, and others should notice! People you care about and trust should confirm this about both of you. As a social being, your discernment of a life partner will affect many people, not just you. It is wise to seek and receive the wisdom of people who love you and want what is best for you.

Second, you will notice that your life plans begin to take your partner into account. This does not mean that either of you gives up completely on all your dreams, and embraces the dreams of the other. But, as you start to feel called to marriage, your deepest desires for yourself will start to include – and even be enhanced and made more exciting by – the dreams and goals that the two of you share. When the dreams for the future that you dream together seem to be more exciting, more fulfilling and more real than the dreams you had for yourself alone, you might be called to marriage.

Finally, if you are called to marriage, the significant commitment of marriage will become very serious. You will notice each other's weaknesses, work on challenges together, and talk about faith, families, money and children, to name a few topics – all to discover if this partnership is really the way God is calling you to serve the world. If you're ready for marriage, you'll be talking a lot about the things that are most important to you.

The above three experiences touch on three significant ways that marriage is different from dating. First, unlike a dating relationship, a marriage relationship is the most significant one in your life. As you seek to become the person God created you to be, your partner should bring out the best in you. Second, while dating people maintain and share separate lives, married people become one flesh. Marriage requires us to travel together, to wait on each other and to be willing to sacrifice ourselves for the other's sake. This is a very important difference; we prepare for it by beginning to share our dreams and vision for the future. Finally, marriage, unlike a dating relationship, is the foundational partnership from which you live your life. Facing challenges together, developing excellent communication skills, and being open and honest with each other prepare you well for marriage. Working together extends into marriage and deepens when you choose to keep loving each other as the challenges you face get more difficult.

Growing in spiritual intimacy

If we have not seen other Christian friends or family in dating relationships, it can be difficult to try to grow in spiritual intimacy. Most of us have very little idea how to go about fostering this growth. Here are a few pointers.

- At first it can be very difficult to pray *with* another person. It's easier to pray *for* each other. Over time, make specific prayer requests to each other when you need extra support.
- Pray together in public, such as before meals with your families. As a couple, go to Mass and other spiritual events involving public prayer.
- Once you are comfortable praying for each other and praying together in public, praying together privately becomes less intimidating. Praying together over a meal when you are alone might be a good way to start. Or, pray a traditional Christian prayer, such as the Our Father or Hail Mary, so you are not trying to think up prayers on the fly.
- As you grow together in all aspects of your relationship, you may feel more comfortable praying together about particular emotional issues that you have shared or current challenges that you are facing.
- Finally, start thinking of prayer as more than just words you say to God together. You can offer your time together to God as a prayer. You can volunteer together to serve your community. Christians are called to offer their whole lives as a prayer to God. The ultimate goal of spiritual intimacy is for married couples to offer their lives to God, who has joined them together. For married people, their marriage is the primary relationship through which God transforms them more and more into holy people!

If you think you might be called to marriage, start asking deeper questions. Seek out the advice of trusted mentors, friends, pastors and family members. Build a network of support that can help you discern your marriage now and support it after you are married, if that's how things turn out. Pray that you will hear God speaking in the voices of those you love, and that God will give you the grace to see clearly. Learn to share your emotions with each other, develop loving habits and cultivate shared interests. Keep dating and start taking seriously the changes that marriage will bring. And take the time you need to be sure that you are making a decision that you can live with – because marriage is not something you can take back!

9

A Spirituality of Marriage

When we first developed our dating model, we looked at the Church's teachings about marriage and asked ourselves how dating might look if it was truly discernment for marriage. Then we each got married and (thankfully) discovered that our dating model had done its job. From the very beginning of our adventure as the "sex-talk people," we insisted that young people need to know something about how the Church understands marriage in order to approach dating appropriately. For many readers, this aspect of romantic relationships may seem a long way off. Even if marriage does not seem like a pressing issue for you right now, it is important to have a basic understanding of Christian marriage. Don't worry if the last couple of chapters sometimes deal with questions you're not dealing with at this time. You can always come back and read them again in a few years.

Most of the Church teaching on marriage focuses on self-giving as it relates to sexual expression in marriage. Obviously, Church teaching on physical intimacy is important, and we'll dedicate the next two chapters to exploring those teachings and the joy we've found in them. One of the richest gifts that the Church's teaching has offered us, however, is that it opens our eyes to the incredible potential of self-giving love in whole people.

Marriage, as a completion of the dating relationship, is the joining of two unique whole persons. Every marriage is different, offering its own unique gift to the world, imaging the self-giving love of the Trinity in its own unique way. When you think about the most amazing marriages you've seen, what qualities in those marriages inspire you? Blake and Brooke are great hosts – they throw amazing parties where families are welcome, the food is spectacular and everyone leaves feeling valued and appreciated. The way their commitment to one another serves their friends, families and neighbours is a wonderful image of a welcoming and hospitable God. Tom and Mary have been married for more than 30 years. Their home is decorated with thousands of love notes written on little cards from flowers, post-it notes and napkins from their years together. They send long, beautiful, handwritten letters to their friends and family. They see God at work in each other and in everyone – and they aren't shy about saying so. Karen and Matthew have had a difficult marriage. One of their children died in childhood in a terrible accident. Matthew struggles with depression, and right from the beginning of the relationship, theirs was an attraction of opposites. Their marriage is one of fierce perseverance. Many times they could have walked away, but their desire to love each other in good times and in bad is making them both better people. Karen and Matthew are a living, breathing sign of how God transforms us in relationship: they are a sign of hope in a broken world.

Human fruitfulness and God's creation

In many ways every day, marriages create a home for God's creation to continue in us as spouses, as children and as members of our communities. Celebrating the gift of our procreative potential by being open to and supportive of children is one of the most profound signs of our love for our Creator God and for a spouse. Parenthood is a sign of and response to God's call for us to be fruitful and multiply, but it is not the only way we are fruitful. We give life to the world when we choose celibacy to serve God's people in religious life. We give life when we allow God's creativity to pour through us when we paint or make music. We give life when we stay committed to difficult and trying relationships, enduring pain for the sake of forgiveness, reconciliation and mercy. We give life when we save money for our children's education, when we give generously to the Church and to charities with our time, talent and treasure, and when we serve Christmas dinner at a soup kitchen. When married people seek expression of their love for one another, it ought to always and everywhere strive to be open to the fullness of life for all of God's people. When this broader view of fruitfulness is kept in mind, discussions between spouses about God's call for their sexual intimacy become part of their discernment of how they will be a part of God's ongoing creation of the kingdom here on earth.

Any adequate spirituality of marriage must understand that marriage is a road to holiness, but maybe not always in the way we imagine. A holy marriage is not a marriage where two people walk around the house constantly saying the Hail Mary and singing hymns (though both of these practices have many benefits, and may be a good tactic for ending an unproductive argument!). Holy practices in marriage include taking out the garbage, cleaning up after yourself and your spouse, and negotiating who will buy groceries and how much to spend. God surprises us by showing up when we're brushing our teeth in the morning, when we are wishing we had just a few more minutes alone together, or when we are washing the car.

Dating (each other) when you are married

Leah's good friend Blake recently wrote an article about how important it is for married couples to date – each other! What a wonderful way to think about things! If dating is a process of discovery – of learning to walk beside and continually learn about this mysterious and beautiful person you love – then marriage is a continuation of that relationship. The potential for growth and depth doesn't end with marriage. Marriage is a new stage of life. Dating when you are married is less a time of preparation and discernment, and more an opportunity for spouses to stay connected and be reminded that their partner is a mystery. If you haven't dated in a healthy way before marriage, dating and continually rediscovering your spouse after marriage might seem an unnecessary chore. A healthy understanding of dating stands you in good stead for maintaining a healthy marriage.

If we approach the Church's teaching on married physical intimacy without seeing the whole of the married adventure as "full of grace," we risk becoming legalistic or reducing our experience of holy marriage to holy sex acts. Marriage is about living social, emotional, intellectual, spiritual and physical intimacy in an exciting journey together.

We cannot expect to have all the answers before we say, "I do." Our partners will change and so will we. The mark of true love is not the absence of change, difficulty or mystery: true love remains faithfully present through all these.

There is something inherently romantic and inspiring about an elderly couple walking through a park holding hands or sneaking a kiss in a grocery store. The physical expression of their love is a sign of a commitment and care that spans decades. Maybe you've been to Mass on a Sunday when the priest calls forward a couple celebrating a sixtieth wedding anniversary and invites them to renew their wedding vows. This liturgical action is a beautiful sign of a holy life together.

When we think about it, liturgical actions make sense because they are signs and images of God's presence that we first experience *outside* the church building. The Eucharist, as sacrifice, feast and communion, makes sense because we watched our parents work to make meals and create a community around the table. We've been fed, as whole people, at countless dinner tables. We've been inspired by these experiences to share them with others. The Liturgy of the Word recounts the stories of people seeking God and God seeking people. The Scriptures read aloud for our hearing make sense because we too are people longing to know God. We have heard God calling us in the encouragement of our parents, friends, and even strangers. We have sensed God's presence in the healing touch of a nurse, in the new growth that follows a forest fire or a series of green lights when we're running late!

Faith makes sense because God is everywhere. Marriage, like the rest of life, is holy ground. We can trust that if God's plan for us includes marriage, we will be truly transformed in our relationship with our spouse, our children and the world. In the context of marriage, sex and physical intimacy become part of the fabric of daily life. Life-giving and redemptive physical intimacy is rooted in the messiness and meaning of dirty laundry waiting to be done, arguments about how to spend money, or the rush to make dinner. Put simply, good and holy physical intimacy, including sex, finds its true meaning in the everyday moments of married relationships.

10

Anything Goes?

Our dating model makes it clear that physical intimacy is an essential part of our relationships with one another, and that physical intimacy is meaningful only in the broader context of our whole relationship with our partner. In marriage, physical intimacy continues be an expression of a whole relationship with another whole person. Couples who learned how to discern their physical intimacy in a healthy way while dating will recognize that we must also think about the broader context for physical intimacy in marriage. Married physical intimacy is not simply about sex, even though the couple is now encouraged to have it. Sex finds its fullest meaning in the context of the whole married life. Imagine a marriage with no physical intimacy *except* for sex. Such a marriage would take sex totally out of context! In such a marriage, sex might not even be an expression of love between the couple, but simply a matter of physical and sexual release.

A recent study indicates that men who contribute more to the household chores enjoy a more active sex life. Why? Helping one's spouse with little daily chores might not seem connected with physical intimacy, but remember, all the different parts of our relationships are connected – or they should be. Any act that makes a spouse feel cared for, appreciated, relieved, rested or understood will contribute to a better married life and to a better sex life. Foreplay helps couples communicate so that sex remains life-giving. Besides setting the mood for sex and preparing the couple's bodies for sex, foreplay tells your spouse that you care for them, that they are not simply a means for your sexual release, that you really want to communicate your whole self to them.

It should be no surprise that the Church not only allows but actually encourages people who have fully committed their lives to one another to have sex. It can take place long before sexual intimacy, perhaps in the form of a note packed into a spouse's lunch or a gift left on a spouse's pillow. Foreplay can be a flirtatious kiss in the morning before work, but it can also be folding the laundry or scrubbing the toilet.

So, married physical intimacy means more than just sex. In determining which actions are appropriate for their marriage, couples cannot rely on the Church for a list of sexual activities that married people are permitted to enjoy. Couples must continue to discern how to communicate their love for one another with their bodies. Sex still needs to be put in its proper context with reference to both a) other expressions of physical intimacy, and b) the marriage relationship as a whole, in its emotional, social, intellectual and spiritual dimensions. How can we do this in a loving and responsible way?

It should be no surprise that the Church believes that people who have fully committed their lives to one another are not only allowed, but actually encouraged, to have sex. Sex expresses the love between spouses, and it also reinforces that love. When sex speaks a language of selfless love, it draws husband and wife closer and closer to each other. The whole point of physical intimacy is to communicate the truth about your relationships using your body. Acts of physical intimacy with your spouse help you communicate about your relationship in ways that can't always be done with just words. A quick kiss as one spouse stays home with the flu is a way for the other to say, "I wish I could spend the day making soup for you and bringing you Kleenex!" A hug offered as one spouse has to leave for work in the middle of an argument is a way to say, "I'm sorry I have to go. I love you even though we're disagreeing about this." At the end of a very long day, with four kids tucked into bed and two full-time jobs set aside for the night, spouses who make love quickly and without words say to one another with the language of their bodies, "I don't have much left, but what I have, I give to you."

In order to be a healthy expression of intimacy, sex must always communicate the truth about the couple's relationship and the truth about sex itself. Because a whole person is social, emotional, spiritual, intellectual and physical, sex between whole people can have many different layers, meanings and consequences. The Catholic tradition has typically talked about two particular consequences of sex – and, by extension, of marriage as a whole – by which we can understand the role of sex within marriage. The first is that sex produces children. This is called the procreative "end" or goal of sex. The second is that sex unifies spouses. This is called the unitive "end" or goal. Any evaluation of sexual morality in marriage – of how to tell the truth with your body – must take these two factors into account.

When we learn to view people as whole people, it becomes clear that these two consequences of sex are interrelated. Sex is unique in its capacity to bring about profound unity between spouses while they participate in God's ongoing creation. The procreative possibility of sex is perhaps the most powerful sign of sex as a source of love, commitment and unity. When couples are blessed with the gift of a new life flowing from their mutual self-gift, their love takes an embodied form in their child. Parents are challenged to become more fully aware that their commitment to one another is also a gift to their children. As we saw earlier in this book, married love is not just for the couple. Married love is for the community, for the building of God's kingdom on earth. As new parents, Brett and Flannery and Leah and Marc are learning that their love for each other is being challenged and deepened by sleepless nights, sick babies and the stress of saving for university education on top of next month's rent and groceries. Babies make their parents (at times, painfully) aware of just how much they need to love each other and be committed and unified. Parenting is a lifelong journey of co-creation with God. An essential aspect of the call to procreation is the call to education. God has entrusted parents with the responsibility to raise children who will live under and contribute to God's reign. This further aspect of education also demands and reinforces the unity of the spouses.

These two "ends" of sex are actually more than interrelated. The Church teaches that the unitive and the procreative aspects of sex are so intricately and necessarily linked that any attitudes or actions that intentionally try to separate them will damage both aspects. In other words, we cannot attempt to disrupt the procreative aspect of sex without also affecting the unitive aspect. This does not mean that Catholics must intend or expect conception to occur each time they make love. After all, there are all kinds of times when the procreative aspect of sex is simply not present: post-menopause, after a hysterectomy, during pregnancy, and roughly 3 out of every 4 weeks in an average menstrual cycle. The Church has no problem with spouses having sex during these times. The problem arises when we try to separate the procreative and the unitive: that is, when we try to alter the nature of sex itself. If we eliminate the procreative aspect when it is naturally present, our unity is impaired. What can this mean?

First of all, it *doesn't* mean that couples who attempt to do this don't love each other. The Church isn't saying that. It is saying that when we try to alter sex and its consequences, our intellectual and emotional attitudes about human fruitfulness and God's generosity are affected. God gives us life without our asking for it, but we are, nevertheless, grateful for the gift. But God didn't give us our lives simply for ourselves. We are called to offer ourselves to others in relationships of love. The life-giving potential in these relationships is not optional – it springs from our creation in God's image. If we are called to marriage, that life-giving potential might be fulfilled by God's gift of children. When we try to eliminate our biological fertility from our actions in sex, we pretend that we are the masters of creation, rather than co-creators with God. We are tempted to stop seeing our gifts of self as being for the sake of the world beyond us, as a privilege and gift from God that we receive with great care and responsibility.

It should be easy to see that any way that we use physical intimacy to lie with our bodies is not okay in marriage (or ever). Couples need to be aware of themselves and what they are trying to communicate with the language of their bodies throughout their marriage relationships. The Church teaches that separating the procreative and unitive aspects of sex damages our relationships by not using our bodies to communicate the truth. With this point in mind, the last part of this chapter will look at two things that can interfere with how spouses express their love for one another honestly and appropriately: mimicking acts and artificial contraception.

1. Mimicking acts

Remember that we mentioned in chapter 3 that acts which mimic sex are not appropriate to dating couples? Any acts with the potential for orgasm are not appropriate for couples who are not married. But for married people who are sharing orgasms together in sex, these acts can be a healthy and creative part of their physical intimacy when used in ways that do not deny the truth about human relationships and sexuality. How can we tell if we are using such acts in a loving way?

We'll look at two points here. The first point should be obvious: no act of intimacy can ever be forced on anyone. Some people may find these acts an exciting addition to their married intimacy, but others may find one or all of them distasteful. If you or your partner does not feel comfortable engaging in a particular act, the other cannot expect it. Normal intercourse is an essential part of the marriage covenant. It cannot be demanded at any time, but it is legitimate for each spouse to expect it from the other in general. This is not the case for acts that mimic sex.

The second point requires a little more thought. The reason these acts do not belong in a dating relationship is that their potential for orgasm means they can have some of the same emotional, social and physical consequences as sex. For this reason, married couples may be tempted to use these acts instead of sex – to avoid pregnancy or to avoid true union. A Catholic understanding of married sexuality insists that, though many acts can be part of a couple's married intimacy, no act can become a replacement for sex, because no other act has the unique combination of procreative and unitive functions that God built into sex. This point can be broken down into two subordinate rules: no act can replace sex in order to avoid the procreative aspect of sex, and no act can replace sex in order to avoid the unitive aspect of sex. If any act is used to avoid either end of sex, spouses are not using that act to honestly express their self-gift to one another.

Unhealthy attitudes towards sex

Two common ways that people have unhealthy attitudes towards sex often show up in the discussion of mimicking acts. The first is that people can act as if there are body parts that are somehow "unfit" or "dirty" for the loving touch of a spouse. However, barring acts that are unhealthy, there is no reason why any particular body part is off-limits. Our bodies – our whole bodies – are God's creation and, as such, good in and of themselves.

The second is a little more complicated. When sex or other acts of physical intimacy do not feel like an expression of love from our spouse, they can lose their appeal very quickly. Spouses who feel used sexually by their partners will enjoy sex less and less. Spouses who constantly or harshly refuse their partners' desires to be sexually intimate can cause both partners to feel isolated or lonely in their marriage. Negative, dishonest, forced or inappropriate sexual expressions can alienate spouses from each other, rather than bringing them closer together.

---

2. *Artificial contraception*

While mimicking acts can be used in a way that is contrary to the truth about human relationships and sexuality, they can have a healthy role in married sexuality. On the other hand, artificial contraception – things like the birth control pill, IUDs, condoms, or spermicidal foam – is never permitted in Catholic teaching. Because these methods are so widely used in our culture, many people struggle to understand what the Church's concerns are with these methods. Some people think that the Church insists that every sexual act must have the potential for conception, but we saw that the Church has no problem with spouses making love at all kinds of times, such as during pregnancy, when conception is not possible. The Church even encourages couples who have good reasons for avoiding pregnancy to plan their families by abstaining from sex when conception appears possible, and engaging in it when conception is not possible. This approach is called Natural Family Planning (NFP), and we will look at it in more detail in the next chapter.

For many people, the Church's distinction between the moral status of NFP and that of artificial contraception is difficult to understand.

"If Catholics have a good reason to avoid pregnancy," they wonder, "then why does the Church care whether they use Natural Family Planning or an artificial means, such as the pill or condoms?" Because this question is so common, we will try to offer a short response here, but we encourage people with concerns about this topic to investigate carefully what the Church teaches in this area and why.

We can start by noting that the question in the previous paragraph presumes that the end justifies the means. In other words, it works on the assumption that if your goal is a good one, then whatever way you try to achieve that goal is also good. The funny thing is that neither the Church nor many people in society accept that reasoning for any other question. We don't accept it for making money, or for losing weight. We don't accept it for winning political office, or for helping the poor. We don't even accept it for getting violent criminals off our streets. According to the moral reasoning used by virtually everyone in society, an act cannot be okay simply because it tries to achieve a goal that is legitimate, or even urgent.

The moral difference between artificial contraception and NFP must lie in how they work, not in what they try to achieve. The real question is "How does artificial contraception function differently than NFP to achieve the same goal?" To put it simply, artificial contraception removes the procreative potential from sex. In doing so, artificial contraception fails to respect the integrity of the persons and their life-giving actions. Natural Family Planning, which can be used both to avoid and to achieve pregnancy, works by teaching couples to engage in their sexual activity with reference to their fertility and God's call to parenthood. When it is used to avoid pregnancy, NFP has the same goal as artificial contraception, but it demands a change in lifestyle. Artificial contraception, meanwhile, hopes to accomplish the same goal with as little reference, or change, to the rest of one's life as possible. One option demands discipline and sacrifice, while the other rejects these attitudes as unnecessarily difficult. In most other areas of life, such as maintaining a healthy weight, it is easy to see that *not* doing things (such as eating junk food) when we don't want their consequences is simply common sense. The Church reminds us that such logic applies to our sex lives as well.

Perhaps the most concise way to express the difference between NFP and artificial contraception is simply this: *NFP alters one's lifestyle to accommodate the nature of sex, while artificial contraception alters the nature of sex to accommodate one's lifestyle.*

When it comes to babies, there are no accidents

Because artificial contraception tries to give us the pleasures of sex without reference to its normal consequences, it subtly teaches us that those normal consequences are not good and healthy. Let's look at one of the most serious problems in our culture that comes from trying to change sex to accommodate our lifestyles.

How does our culture refer to children who were conceived despite the best efforts of artificial birth control? Often, we call them "accidents." Now, what on earth can this mean? You can crash your car by accident, you can lock your keys in your house by accident, you can burn dinner by accident, but you can't make a baby by accident. We know exactly what makes babies. If you do it and you get pregnant, it is not an accident. Babies are not the flu. You can't "catch" pregnancy. Pregnancy is a sign that everything is working the way it should. Accidents are the opposite of that. The fact that we are willing to refer to little people as "accidents" shows that trying to eliminate the procreative aspect of sex distorts our understanding of what sex is and what sex does.

By altering the way society thinks about sex, artificial contraception has blurred the connection between sex and babies in the minds of many people. Couples using NFP, on the other hand, are intimately aware that sex leads to babies. They are confronted, every month, with the possibility of having sex during a time when conceiving a baby is a very distinct possibility. Couples using NFP know the truth about sex and act accordingly. And they know that babies are never accidents.

We have all grown up in a society that takes artificial birth control for granted. People who raise questions about it are often portrayed as the "fun police" who just need to catch up with the times. Many of us have never seriously asked ourselves about the moral implications of artificial contraception. Questioning our assumptions about artificial contraception is part of a long conversion process. If you have never had the Church's teaching on artificial contraception explained to you, we hope you're feeling inspired to do some more research and reading, and to ask some more questions.

By the way, just because the Church does not support artificial contraception doesn't mean you are expected to have 25 kids! See Chapter 11 for the Church's approach to planning your family.

When contraceptives are used to treat other health conditions

Though the Church is against the use of artificial contraception as a contraceptive, there is no teaching against the use of hormonal methods as medications for other conditions. The pill may be prescribed for heavy, painful menstruation, for acne, for ovarian disorders, or to restart menstruation following radiation treatments or any number of other illnesses. In such cases, these pills might not be serving as contraceptives. The problem emerges when women are using these treatments for illness and they might also be acting as contraceptives. If you find yourself in one of these situations, find a doctor who is sympathetic to your desire to avoid hormonal birth control if there are other options. And talk to someone you trust in the Church about how you can respond both to God's call to health and to open, honest, life-giving intimacy with your spouse.

Even though there are some circumstances where a drug that doubles as birth control can be a woman's best medical option, birth control is hugely overprescribed. Pharmaceutical companies are happy about that: if a young woman can be put on the pill for acne when she's 14, she might be a customer for decades. But hormonal birth control has many potential side effects, and some can intensify with long-term use. If you don't want to be on the pill when you are married, you'll need to find alternative therapies anyway. Young women should not let their doctors put them on the pill unless they are convinced that it is absolutely necessary.

11

What Is NFP, Anyway?

We learned in the last chapter that the Church teaches that spouses are called to responsible parenthood, but rejects the use of artificial contraception. How are Catholic couples to plan their families? The Church's answer is NFP, or Natural Family Planning. Since most of us do not learn about NFP in school or from our doctor, we're going to spend this chapter giving you some basic information about it. Please be aware that reading this chapter does not qualify you to practise or teach NFP. If you choose to use NFP now or in the future, you will have to study the method(s) in more detail than we can present here.

So, what is NFP anyway? Well, it is a lot of different things. It is an inexpensive, safe, natural, healthy and morally responsible alternative to artificial contraception. It is an effective way to achieve pregnancy for couples who struggle with infertility. And it is a way of living married life that has numerous practical benefits for relationships. But, more than any of these things, *NFP is a form of Christian discipleship.* We will deal with the other issues in our list in the rest of this chapter, but their full importance will be missed if we do not first address the key issue of NFP as discipleship.

As you are aware by now, Christian ethics cannot be reduced to simply doing the right thing or the wrong thing. The fundamental concern that sets the context for all of our individual choices about right and wrong is "What kind of person am I becoming? A person of virtue?" It is even possible to do the right thing for the wrong reason. When we do that, we are not becoming people of virtue. Christians are called to allow Christ to form them into people of virtue so that choosing the good becomes a matter of habit. When we choose to follow Jesus, our whole lives should look different. We are called to take up our cross and follow him. We might approach our jobs differently, and spend our money and time differently. We recognize that we are part of the human family and are obligated to ask not just "What should I do?" but also "What are my actions doing to the people around me?"

In the last chapter, we noted that the major difference between NFP and artificial contraception is that NFP tries to integrate family planning into a whole lifestyle. Because artificial contraception separates sex from its normal consequences, it also separates sex from the rest of our lives. When people use artificial contraception, it can become difficult for them to see how sexual behaviour reflects the rest of their relationship. But for any physical intimacy to be healthy and fulfilling, it must be integrated with the rest of our relationship. In the context of marriage, NFP is a form of discipleship that helps us see how sex relates to the rest of our lives.

If we are going to understand how all this works on a practical level, we need to spend a little time looking at the basics of NFP. How does it work and what does that mean for the lifestyles of those who practise it?

We've already mentioned that that no one has a whole reproductive system. What we have is *half* a reproduction system. To make a baby, you need to cooperate with another person who has the other half. A man's half of this system is always turned on. Once he has reached sexual maturity, if a man remains healthy, he can always participate in making a baby. A woman's half of the system is a little more complicated. For most of the time, women are not fertile. A woman can get pregnant only for a few days each month, surrounding ovulation (when her body releases an egg cell). NFP allows couples to determine when the woman is ovulating. If they are avoiding pregnancy, they refrain from sex during this time. If they are trying to achieve pregnancy, they engage in sex at this time. In this way, couples can use NFP to plan their families.

So, how can a woman and her partner figure out when she is ovulating? As you are probably aware, a woman's body goes through a cycle each month that determines her fertility. Once a month a woman ovulates. If the egg is not fertilized, it leaves her body, along with blood and the lining of her uterus that had built up, just in case, to feed a tiny baby. This discharge is the woman's period. What you may not know is that a woman's body gives all kinds of little hints, or indicators, that will tell the observant woman or couple where she is in her cycle and, most importantly, when she is ovulating. Most people already look for bodily hints for other situations – a fever, runny nose or cough tells you that you may have a cold or the flu. If we learn to understand the body's reproductive hints, we can tell with remarkable accuracy when sex might lead to pregnancy and when it won't.

There are many different methods of natural family planning. The difference between them is usually a matter of which fertility indicators they focus on. Which one is best for you depends on which indicators are easiest for you to follow. This varies from woman to woman. Some methods focus on temperature, because a woman's body cools off slightly just before she ovulates in order to be a hospitable home for sperm, which like it just a little cooler than normal body temperature. (That's why men keep them on the outside.) Some focus on vaginal mucus, which changes over the course of the month from a sperm blocker, when a woman is infertile, to a sperm super-highway, when she is ovulating. Some of the more high-tech methods measure a woman's hormone balance in order to determine her fertility, a little like a home pregnancy test. Many methods use more than one indicator to make sure the reading you are getting is as accurate as possible. To find out which is the best for you, research all of them and talk to a doctor who specializes in NFP or to a certified NFP teacher. NFP is most effective when a couple works closely with an experienced NFP teacher.

Getting started with NFP

Learning how to use NFP can take a little time and practice. It's a good idea to start looking into it as soon as marriage becomes a serious possibility for you, or even sooner. Having your chosen method down pat before you start having sex makes everything run much more smoothly. It can also help you to tell which NFP method works best for you.

No form of family planning is statistically perfect, but these methods are comparable to the most effective forms of artificial contraception, with studies indicating success rates in the 95% to 99% range. Sometimes you will hear that natural family planning is ineffective for preventing pregnancy, but this is usually misinformation based on the old "rhythm method," where couples used a calendar to give them an informed guess at the woman's fertility. It worked at a rate of about 75%.

Another statistic about NFP is even more surprising. Most studies indicate that couples using NFP have divorce rates of less than 5%! And this is in a culture where the divorce rate in general, and even among other religious people, is around 50%. This statistic alone makes looking into natural family planning worth your time.

So, why do couples who use NFP have better success rates in terms of lasting marriages?

If the basic premise of this book makes sense – that is, if physical intimacy that tells the truth about our relationships is healthier and holier – it shouldn't be a big surprise that NFP has many practical benefits. Let's look at a few:

• *NFP is a constant reminder that our sexuality is not just about us.* Because every decision NFP requires is made with full awareness about the consequences of sex, NFP teaches us to recognize that every move we make affects others. Though our sexual intimacy with our spouse is deeply sacred and mostly private, our sexuality impacts the world. It also draws us into the world, helping us to recognize Christ in every person and in all of creation.

• *NFP encourages both partners to be responsible for family planning.* NFP fosters a shared responsibility for family planning, inviting both husband and wife to take up the call to responsible parenthood. While many artificial methods place the burden of these decisions solely on the woman, the decision to abstain from sex requires mutual support and the self-control of both parties.

• *NFP is natural.* The most common forms of birth control in our society involve a woman taking synthetic hormones, via pills, patches, needles or vaginal inserts. Women in our society are taking so many synthetic hormones (such as estrogen) that male fish swimming downstream from human sewage are developing female anatomy! If we found these kinds of hormones in our milk at the supermarket, the public outcry would be immense, but a huge number of women voluntarily take them daily. NFP, on the other hand, does nothing to alter a woman's body. It works by observing a woman's fertility, not manipulating it.

• NFP respects women. It values the unique and miraculous process of ovulation and conception without manipulating a woman's body. Many women find the side effects of hormonal birth control – things like weight gain, increased irritability, loss of interest in sex, even blood clots – such a burden that they stop using it within a few months. From a medical perspective, NFP is perfectly safe. In fact, it's more than safe. Because it requires such detailed knowledge about the woman's body, some women have found out about other health issues long before these would have been discovered by other means.

• *NFP helps couples grow closer sexually.* Just like healthy asceticism (such as giving up chocolate or sleeping in for Lent) can teach us the value of the item or practice we abstain from, periodically abstaining from sex can help couples value and honour their deep and meaningful sexual relationship.

• *NFP is practically free.* The birth control industry is a perfect example of consumerism gone wrong. It takes something that no one needs, convinces people that they need it, and then sits back and watches the money roll in. Couples who use NFP spend a small amount of money buying a thermometer or fertility monitor at the beginning. Sometimes instruction is free and sometimes there is a fee. Sometimes couples buy a book. After these start-up costs, your biggest expense is a pencil and paper for keeping track of your symptoms.

• *NFP encourages communication between couples.* Babies affect every aspect of a couple's life together. Couples using NFP to avoid pregnancy are reminded each month of their decision. Sometimes this reminder comes as an invitation to revisit the question. When couples talk regularly about whether or not to add to their family, those conversations will have to cover every other aspect of their lives together. Even if they aren't being called to add to their family, God uses NFP to remind them of other ways their marriages are called to be life-giving. Let's listen in on Brad and Maria:

Communicating about our marriage and our call to co-creation

Maria: I really wish we could make love tonight, Brad. It's so frustrating that we can't right now. Are we sure we aren't ready for another baby?

Brad: Well, we've been talking about making sure that we have enough time to help Greg manage his learning disability now that he's in school. Could we do that with another child? Anna's three-year-old energy is already distracting for him ...

Maria: Yeah, I'm not sure we could. At least not right now – I've got enough on my hands with the two of them. We'd also have to stop coordinating marriage preparation for the next couple of years if we had another baby right now. And my sister and Mike are taking the program next fall. I think our presence could really help them understand the spiritual elements of marriage.

Brad: I hadn't thought about that. Oh – and I'm sorry I've been leaving all the work with the kids to you lately. Tonight, after you worked all day, I let you make dinner even though the kids were pleading for your attention. I shouldn't just sit there reading the newspaper when you need a hand.

Maria: (cuddling up to Brad on the couch) Thanks for noticing. I didn't want to say anything in front of the kids.

Brad: (giving her a kiss) By the way, at marriage prep last night, you did a great job talking about how married life is a lifetime of discovering more about your partner ...

So, NFP has a lot of practical benefits for married life. Great. Now let's look a little closer. Benefits such as being low-cost are nice, but the majority of benefits are of a different sort. The benefits that NFP brings to marriages don't happen by magic. If you look carefully, you'll see that the reason NFP has most of the benefits we listed is because it makes real demands of the people who use it. Like most things in life, good marriages require a lot of hard work and commitment. NFP is not a substitute for that. It has these practical benefits for marriages because it is a constant incentive to work hard. It requires mutual sacrifice and discipline to achieve a common goal. The low divorce rate of NFP users seems to indicate that mutual sacrifice and discipline to achieve a common goal is really good for relationships.

NFP is more than just another method of family planning. It is a lifestyle, a way of being present to your own body and self, and being present and responsive to your spouse. It involves abstaining from sex for (on average) about a week every month (and sometimes longer, such as after a baby is born, or during times of illness). For these reasons, NFP requires patience, understanding and the willingness to talk to your spouse about your sexual desires and intimacy.

These considerations are what we mean to emphasize when we say that NFP needs to be understood, first and foremost, as a form of Christian discipleship. NFP is not a cure-all that will automatically give you a perfect married life together. Christian discipleship is not designed to lead you to a comfortable life, though it is designed to lead to true happiness. People who have chosen the path of Christian discipleship know that the good life and the easy life are not the same thing.

NFP is a safe and healthy way to plan a family. It encourages self-control and mutual respect. It reinforces the value of children and keeps the spouses aware that every time they have sex, they are being called out of themselves. But it is not always easy. At times it is a sacrifice, an instance of spiritual and physical discipline, an exercise of obedience and a cross of Christian discipleship. We should not shy away from it just because it has its challenges. Challenges can be tremendous opportunities for growth.

For many people, NFP works according to plan: if you have discerned that God is not calling you to have a child at this point, you refrain from intercourse for about one week each month. Beyond that week, your sex life continues normally. For other people, NFP can be more challenging. Couples who have started with a method that is not the best one for them can have a difficult time discerning the woman's fertility. Other issues, such as the disruption of a woman's normal cycle by injury or illness, can also make fertility tough to discern. Most couples using NFP will tell you that the hardest time to figure out if a woman is ovulating is after she has a baby. Some women don't ovulate for many months after giving birth, while others start up again right away. Women with erratic cycles can use NFP effectively, but it usually takes longer to master the method.

All these situations require more self-control from both spouses. When you can't read fertility, you can do one of two things: have sex knowing that you might get pregnant, or refrain until you can get an accurate reading. Both can bring a certain anxiety to sexual intimacy.

Many groups in the Church do good work by educating people about NFP. Too often, however, they tend to present NFP as a cure-all for marital trouble. Some have even gone so far as to say that Catholic couples would have no troubles in marriage if they all used NFP. Not only is this view incorrect, it is quite dangerous.

If NFP is presented as a cure-all rather than a form of discipleship, there is no mention of the difficulties that some couples can have. When a couple has been taught about NFP as if it were simply a Catholic form of birth control, but full of magic benefits, they can be surprised when they struggle with NFP in their marriage. This can lead to unnecessary guilt because they feel like they must be doing something wrong. This guilt can keep them from talking to other Catholics who might be in the same situation. Couples who struggle with NFP can feel isolated when everyone around them is raving about NFP's benefits. If you ever struggle with NFP, know that you are not alone. You have not done anything wrong. You are being formed into disciples of Christ, and that is not always easy. Don't suffer in silence because you feel guilty. Contact a certified teacher. In most cases, they will be able to help you get a better read on your fertility and work through any anxiety. Make advance plans with your teacher if you know you will be entering a time when NFP is more complicated, such as after a baby or during menopause. There are people who can help you when NFP gets tough.

The role of the community of faith is to support people who are struggling with the difficulties of Christian discipleship, not to isolate them. Rather than suggesting that NFP is a magic solution to marital difficulty, those who promote it serve the Church better by using their ministry to help people who struggle with NFP.

Serious reasons and responsible parenthood

The Catholic Church teaches that it can be morally legitimate to avoid pregnancy, but not that it is morally legitimate to avoid pregnancy whenever you feel like it. At a Catholic wedding, spouses make the solemn vow to accept children lovingly from God. This openness is an essential part of Christian marriage. Still, the Church teaches that we are called to *responsible* parenthood. Most couples in our society can't responsibly have a baby every year. In order for the decision to avoid pregnancy to be morally justified, couples need a serious reason. What exactly does this mean?

Our call in marriage is to be life-giving; this cannot be avoided or put off indefinitely for selfish or flippant reasons. Some common serious reasons for avoiding pregnancy include financial hardship, health concerns associated with pregnancy, physical and emotional exhaustion, lack of adequate housing, uncertain employment, age, psychological issues, government restrictions, and a threatened ability to meet the needs of children the couple already has.

The Church is clear that the parents, and only the parents, are responsible for decisions about family planning. While the general encouragement to be open to life and the celebration of large families are perfectly legitimate, people outside the marriage who cannot know the intimate details of a family's life together must refrain from judging a couple's decision not to add to their family.

Issues such as finances or reproductive and psychological health are private. Couples who are struggling with infertility can be especially hurt by comments that they should be having children. Accusations that someone else's reasons for avoiding pregnancy are not serious enough must be avoided.

Couples who are avoiding pregnancy must carefully examine their situation and know in their consciences that such a decision is not made for selfish reasons. To find the answer to this question, couples may want to talk to their pastor, friends and family, or other couples in similar situations. They will also want to talk to God in prayer. Couples should revisit the question of avoiding or welcoming a pregnancy when their serious situation changes. NFP encourages couples to discern regularly whether God is calling them to add to their family.

12

God Gave You a Conscience

Following your conscience is the highest moral teaching in the Catholic Church. St. Thomas Aquinas is famous for teaching that a person must follow his or her conscience, even if that conscience is in error. Any Catholic book that deals with moral teachings of the Church must therefore address the question of conscience. Because this important teaching is often misused in the area of sexuality, it is especially important for us here.

Now, why on earth would St. Thomas tell us we must follow a conscience that is in error? Remember what we have mentioned over and over in this book: living the moral life is not simply about doing the right thing, as important as that is, but it is about becoming the right kind of person. St. Thomas is insisting that the first requirement of Christian living is being formed into a disciple of Christ. When we choose how to act in a given situation, we must always do what we think is right in that situation. But how will we know what is right? We must become people of virtue who, when faced with a tough situation, will habitually know the right thing to do and have the courage and the grace to do it. Thomas's point, then, is to emphasize the importance of formation, not to neglect the importance of doing the right thing.

The Christian life is all about growing in virtue. We cannot ever act against our conscience. But, if we take care to grow as Christ's disciples and as people of virtue, who invest our time and energy into learning how to act out of love in each situation, we can trust that our consciences will not lead us astray.

The Church has called this aspect of growth in Christian discipleship the "formation of conscience." Because you must follow your
conscience when faced with a particular situation, it is essential that
you form your conscience. We will look at how Catholics can form
their consciences properly, but first we must look at two ways this
teaching is often misinterpreted:

1) Following your conscience means you can do whatever you
like.

2) A properly formed conscience necessarily agrees with the
Church, so you must simply submit, without question, to the
Church in every circumstance.

Both of these models are *exactly* wrong and, though they look
like opposites, they are wrong for exactly the same reason. Church
teaching on the primacy of conscience emphasizes that every human
being is ultimately responsible for themselves and their moral decisions. At the root of both of the above models of conscience is one
thing: abdicating or not taking personal responsibility when it comes
to moral decision making.

At first glance it may be less clear that the first model is an abdi-
cation of responsibility. The second model is easier to understand in
this way, because it is clear to whom you are abdicating your responsibility – the Church. But what about the first model? If you simply
do whatever you like, you are abdicating your responsibility to almost
anything – any passing fancy, any fleeting impulse, any peer pressure,
any hope that nothing really bad will come of it, any rationalization
that you can do evil so something good may come of it.

Think about the last time your conscience really held you ac-
countable for something. You did something, and you knew it was
wrong – not because you were afraid of getting caught, not because
it came back to bite you, but simply because you knew it was wrong.
Got one now? As you think about this experience, you will realize that
your conscience is not something that confirms every decision and
impulse. It is that voice inside us that says we can't always do whatever we want. A model of conscience that suggests that doing what I
want is the same thing as doing what my conscience says destroys any
meaningful understanding of conscience. So, even more obviously, is

a model that says, "Obey without questioning." In any case, there are all kinds of questions where the Church has no concrete teaching to obey, such as when a first kiss should happen, how old people should be before they start dating, or which political party to vote for. But if you've formed your conscience, you will be well prepared to deal with these kinds of issues.

So, how do you go about properly forming your conscience?

In the vast majority of cases, our conscience agrees with Church teaching before we have even heard it. We know that murdering, lying, stealing, cheating and a whole lot of other things are wrong without the Church having to tell us. The heart of the matter is this: "What should we do when we find Church teaching that does not match up with our conscience?"

The question of artificial contraception has triggered many discussions about the role of conscience. We will refer to it below, but you can apply these basic principles to any question your conscience is exploring.

Step 1: Find out what *the Church actually teaches.* This may seem obvious, but many Catholics reject Church teaching without knowing what that teaching is. For example, many people think that the Church teaches that couples can use no form of family planning and must have as many children as possible. Some people think the Church allows no form of *effective* family planning. Others think Catholic couples are expected to have sex only when they are actively trying to conceive a child. None of these points are true, but such impressions exist in numerous variations both inside and outside the Catholic community.

Knowing exactly what the Church teaches means taking the time to read official Church teaching and talk with people who understand and live it. For most topics, information is available in the *Catechism of the Catholic Church.* If you have read the Catechism and are not exactly sure what it says about the topic you are interested in, go to someone you know and trust who is faithful to Church teaching, such as a pastor, teacher or family member. Work through the issue with them, making sure that you understand just what the Church says.

Step 2: Find out why *the Church teaches what it does.* Some people think the Church forbids artificial birth control because every single sexual act must have the possibility of conception. But that can't be why the Church is against artificial birth control. If it were, the Church would also be against sex during pregnancy, sex after menopause, and sex after hysterectomies or certain injuries. This approach would even rule out the responsible use of natural family planning, in which couples seek to have sex when conception is not possible. As we saw in Chapter 10, the Church forbids none of these things.

While the Catechism gives us the "what" about most Catholic teaching, it is relatively brief when dealing with the "why." If you understand the "what," but the "why" is still bothering you, you will have to study Church teaching more intensely. There are many good books written on almost every topic of our faith. Try to find books that explain Church teaching in a clear and comprehensive way. You may want to ask Catholics you know and trust to recommend books on particular topics. Also, talk to your pastor or other people in leadership in your faith community who are equipped to deal with your question in a detailed way. Don't give up too early. If you are serious about properly forming your conscience, make sure you are reading the best the Church has to offer. Don't let one bad book or one uninformed person in leadership throw you off.

Finally, any person who is struggling with understanding or accepting a particular Church teaching needs to pray about it. This is not a trivial add-on. If the real goal of the Christian life is becoming better disciples of Jesus, then we need to talk to him. Ask for the gift of understanding. Ask to be led to someone who can help explain the things that confuse you. Pray over the passage in a book that you can't quite wrap your head around. Tell God exactly what it is you don't understand. Tell God why you think you might be struggling. Ask God to show you what other issues in your life might be involved in the specific issue that is bothering you.

For many people, knowing what the Church teaches and understanding the reason for the teaching is enough. Having responsibly pursued these questions, they find that their conscience is in accord with the teaching of the Church. They are comfortable making the resulting moral decisions. (They are also well prepared to discern God's call in related situations where there is no concrete Church teaching.) Much of the confusion in the Church about artificial contraception would be cleared up if Catholics simply followed these first two steps.

Step 3: What to do if you cannot accept a particular teaching. Some Catholics who have responsibly followed the first two steps still find themselves at odds with Church teaching on a given issue. They can still be Catholics in good standing, but they must act responsibly. First, they must not treat the Church or the teaching in question with contempt, such as by publicly mocking the teaching or using parishes, schools or other educational structures to undermine the teaching of the Church in the minds of those who are being formed in the faith. Second, they must be willing to revisit the question when presented with new arguments or situations. A Catholic can say, "I find that I cannot submit to the teaching of the Church on this issue," but a Catholic cannot say, "I will never submit to the teaching of the Church on this issue." The possibility that you are in error must be left open, even if you don't expect to change your mind.

The final question for the person still in disagreement with Church teaching after sincerely trying to form their conscience is "How must I act in this particular situation?" If the person simply has not been fully convinced of a specific Church teaching, it is still possible to follow that teaching. A person doesn't need to be fully convinced that the Church is correct in every detail in order to follow Church teaching in good conscience. If, on the other hand, the person is convinced that following Church teaching in a particular situation would be sinful, they must *not* follow Church teaching. This is a far cry from deciding which Church teachings to follow based on personal preference, or opting out because certain arguments are not fully accepted. The true essence of Church teaching on conscience is that it is never okay to do what you believe to be sinful.

Conclusion

God Calls *All* of You: Sexuality and Vocation ⟲

Living in the midst of a culture obsessed with sex (in music, movies, advertising, conversation, and even the children's sections of clothing stores), it is at times all too easy to define our whole selves by our sexual activity or choices. We can place too much value on our relationship status on Facebook. We can become so obsessed about maintaining our own purity with reference to others' impurity that our sexual activity (or lack of it) becomes our identity. We can end up thinking more about what a couple was doing for an hour alone on Saturday night than the incredible gift their relationship is to their families and communities. Christian faith makes us aware that sexuality is about more than dating and physical intimacy. We are called as whole persons, mysterious and unique beings, created in the image and likeness of God, to be disciples of Jesus Christ.

The invitation to follow Jesus is an adventure filled with the unknown. But we do know that it will consist of relationships with other people created and called by God. When Jesus asks the rich young man to sell everything he has and give it to the poor, the man is devastated. When Jesus reminds us that in order to gain our lives, we have to lose them, it's not surprising that we're tempted to hold on to what we've got!

Christianity is a radical and often counter-cultural way of living. In the Western world, one of the most defining questions we ask ourselves is "What do I want to be when I grow up?" A more fitting question for Christians is "Who is God calling me to become?" When it comes to discerning Christian relationships, the question "How far can we go?" is another way of asking, "How am I being called to give of myself in relationships?" Asking the question this way is a reminder that my sexuality is about my whole self in relation to other people and to God's work in me.

Becoming holy is not about living a life of sterile piety in a hermitage: saints are made in the living of life! *Your life is holy ground and you are called to sainthood.* As a young person, you are probably still waiting to see what lifestyle vocation God has in mind for you. Discerning your life's vocation will not be the end of God's work – it will be a joyful beginning! So keep your eyes, ears and heart wide open.

Life is about being transformed into saints. The best preparation for whatever vocation God has in mind for you will be to enter into each new relationship trusting that God is waiting inside every person you meet to surprise and transform you. Maybe you'll start dating a great girl or guy tomorrow who will become a spouse who, in the end, helps you learn patience. But we must also understand our sexuality more broadly. Perhaps this summer you will develop a friendship with an elderly man on the daily bus to work during a summer job in a new city. Maybe next week your life will be forever changed by witnessing two small children reunited with a parent in a train station. In several years, you might name your firstborn child after a monk who taught you Italian in a monastery while you were travelling. Maybe your experience of parents who loved each other deeply will inspire you to offer your life to serve families through a religious vocation.

Try not to worry too much about whether your vocation is to marriage, single life or religious life. Trust that God will show you the next step when you need to take it. Living life and relationships in joyful expectation is great preparation for your life's calling, whatever that might be. If you learn to live in this way, it will bear much fruit in your more permanent vocation to single, religious or married life.

As we grow into discerning people, we become more aware that God is constantly calling us. We become more aware of how God creates us for human relationships as we find affirmation, hope, inspiration and love in those around us. This is how we become mature in our sexuality: we hear God calling us to relationships and we say "yes" in a way that changes us and changes the world!

Mary's "yes" to God is a perfect example. It is a gift to the world. In fact, Mary is the model of Christian discipleship because her "yes" is so complete. When Gabriel asks her to be the mother of Christ, she says, "I am the servant of the Lord. May it be done to me according to your word." Mary's particular vocation is a "yes" to motherhood. Through her gifts of self in caring for her son and sharing him with the world, she participates in his gift of himself to the world – the gift that ultimately saves us all. Mary's openness to God's presence was expressed through her openness to Joseph, Jesus, her family, her neighbours, the disciples and the Church. All of these relationships brought her ever closer to the God she loved – precisely through her vocation to discipleship, marriage and parenthood. Mary's "yes" – indeed, a lifetime of saying "yes" – was an act and an attitude that changed her and changed the world. Your "yes" will, too.

You are called beyond yourself into relationships that will change and challenge you – and where you will change and challenge others. Dating relationships are just one set of relationships in which we strive to give of ourselves and receive the gifts of others. As we participate in God's creation – through generosity, service, art, true listening, ensuring that no one walks alone, and the countless other ways that we can be the hands and feet of Jesus in the world – our whole selves are taken up in the work of God.

Our prayer is that this book is a reminder that God is chasing you, longing to love you and to help you experience his love in relationships with his people. Your role is to walk carefully on this holy ground, hoping and even expecting to find God everywhere. We are praying that God will guide you clearly and with great joy to work at relationships that will build God's kingdom here on earth.

May your relationships with your friends, family and community be sources of God's many gifts to you. May you encounter Jesus in the people who cross your path as you discern your vocation. And may every relationship of your life be a gift to you and to others!